Always Get the Name of the Dog

D0061273

Always Get the Name of the Dog is a guide to journalistic interviewing, written by a journalist, for journalists. It features advice from some of the best writers and reporters in the business, and takes a comprehensive view of media interviewing across multiple platforms, while emphasizing active learning to give readers actionable steps to become great media interviewers. Through real scenarios and examples, this text takes future journalists through the steps of the interview, from research to source identification to question development and beyond. Whether you are a journalism student or an experienced reporter looking to sharpen your skills, this text can help make sure you get all you need from every interview you conduct.

Nicole Kraft Ed.D. is a professor of journalism at The Ohio State University, and has been a professional journalist and writer for decades.

Always Get the Name of the Dog

A Guide to Media Interviewing

Nicole Kraft Ed.D.

Routledge
Taylor & Francis Group

NEW YORK AND LONDON

First published 2019
by Routledge
711 Third Avenue, New York, NY 10017

and by Routledge
2 Park Square, Milton Park, Abingdon, Oxon, OX14 4RN

Routledge is an imprint of the Taylor & Francis Group, an informa business

© 2019 Taylor & Francis

Library of Congress Cataloging-in-Publication Data
Names: Kraft, Nicole, author.
Title: Always get the name of the dog : a guide to media
interviewing / Nicole Kraft.
Description: New York, NY : Routledge, 2019.
Identifiers: LCCN 2018032893| ISBN 9780815370727 (hardback) |
ISBN 9780815370734 (paperback) | ISBN 9781351248754 (ebk)
Subjects: LCSH: Interviewing in journalism. |
Interviewing in mass media.
Classification: LCC PN4784.I6 K73 2019 | DDC 070.4/3--dc23
LC record available at https://lccn.loc.gov/2018032893

ISBN: 978-0-815-37072-7 (hbk)
ISBN: 978-0-815-37073-4 (pbk)
ISBN: 978-1-351-24875-4 (ebk)

Typeset in Bembo
by Integra Software Services Pvt. Ltd.

To Brian and Danny
For any question, the answer is always
"... because I love you."

Contents

List of Boxes   viii
Acknowledgments   ix

Introduction: Welcome to the Conversation   1

1   Success Starts with Research   6

2   Something about Sources   16

3   Getting it Down   34

4   Location Matters   44

5   Questions and Answers   57

6   Tricks of the Talking Trade   76

7   Covering Sports   92

8   Speeches, Press Conference and Meetings, Oh My   109

9   Interviewing across Media   114

10 Ethics of Interviewing   123

11 There Are Stupid Questions—But You Don't Have to Ask Them   136

12 Let's Talk   151

Resources   *155*
Index   *158*

Boxes

1.1	How Much Reporting Is Enough?	10
1.2	Hi Columbus—It's Me, Summer	13
2.1	When Less Is More	18
2.2	The Police Chase	19
2.3	Second-Grade Source	23
2.4	Begin with the Pitch	29
2.5	Unnamed Sources	31
4.1	Report, Write, Rewrite	53
5.1	"He Remembers It All"	57
5.2	When "What Was in Your Mind" Goes Wrong	63
5.3	Carving Out Character in 30 Questions	65
5.4	Getting Past the Script	71
5.5	How Do You Ask That?	73
6.1	Five Steps to an Intimate Interview	80
6.2	Walking through Time and Memory	84
6.3	"Your Job There Is to Listen"	88
7.1	Vardon Explains His Jersey	97
7.2	Reporting on Player Time	99
9.1	Greasing the Conversation	117
10.1	Code of Ethics	124
10.2	Victim Interviews	127
10.3	It's about Truth and Facts	131
11.1	Anatomy of an Interview	142

Acknowledgments

I am grateful to all my friends, and fellow journalists and educators who shared their time and resources to make this book come to life, including:

Collin Binkley, Associated Press Boston

Matt Brown, associate director of college brands for SB Nation

Summer Cartwright, Lantern campus editor, *Columbus Dispatch* digital news desk intern, *Ohio State Lantern* alum

Chris Davey, associate vice president of Communications at The Ohio State University

Lane DeGregory, staff writer at *Tampa Bay Times*

Bill Finley, sports writer

Steve Fox, sports writer and journalism faculty at the University of Massachusetts at Amherst

Jo Ingles, reporter at Ohio Public Radio/TV

Sally Kuzemchak, magazine writer and Real Mom Nutrition blogger

Charles Leerhsen, former executive editor, *Sports Illustrated*, author of *Blood and Smoke: A True Tale of Mystery, Mayhem and the Birth of the Indy 500* and *Ty Cobb: A Terrible Beauty*

Randy Ludlow, senior reporter at the *Columbus Dispatch*

Alison Lukan, *The Athletic Columbus*

Mac McClelland, reporter featured in *New York Times Magazine, Rolling Stone, San Francisco Magazine, New York Magazine*

Paul Oren, sports writer and lecturer at Valparaiso University

Jeff Pearlman, sports writer and *New York Times* best-selling author

Dan Plesac, former Major League pitcher, Major League Baseball Network analyst

Sarah Saffian, magazine journalist, author of *Ithaka: A Daughter's Memoir of Being Found*

Lori Schmidt, sports radio personality

Brittany Schock, reporter

Jennifer Smith-Richards, data reporter at *Chicago Tribune*

Lynn Sygiel and the wonderful students of **Y-Press**

Cory Tressler, Ohio State Digital First, Director of Learning Programs & Digital Flagship at The Ohio State University

WEWS ABC 5, Cleveland

Tom Withers, Cleveland-area sports writer for the Associated Press

Holly Zachariah, *Columbus Dispatch* reporter

Introduction

Welcome to the Conversation

It was a complicated story of a death in southern Ohio.

Four people murdered by a friend who shot everyone in the family, including the dog. The suspect then drove to Columbus, Ohio, and got into a gunfight with police officers.

The convoluted situation required reporter Collin Binkley, then with the *Columbus Dispatch*, to reach out to officials across multiple jurisdictions for the information he needed. He conducted nearly a dozen interviews and obtained quotes from family, witnesses and police. He reported the circumstances of the crime, the suspect and the surroundings.

After hours of interviewing and writing, Binkley called in his story, every fact painstakingly reported. The news desk, however, requested one key, missing fact:

"What was the name of the dog?"

Most of us think interviews are simply asking questions and getting answers, but true interview skills come from asking the right questions of the right sources, and gathering all of the information your reader need and wants to know.

An interview can be defined as an interaction involving dialogue between two people, where questions are asked to elicit information. They actually take place every day to transmit information, be it socially, formally or in business. And that is why journalists use interviews every day to find and report the news that keeps a society informed.

If that sounds like a conversation, good, because that is the fundamental structure of an interview done well.

Too often journalists view interviews solely as the time and space in which to ask questions they have jotted into a notebook. That is a logical but superficial view. The quality and useful end product of an interview comes from a lengthy equation combining:

- Understanding of your story.
- Researching of the facts of your story.
- Determining what information you need for that story.
- Determining what exact sources you need to get that information.

Figure 0.1 Asking questions in an interview means thinking of every fact the reader might need to know—including the name of the dog.

Source: Creative Commons/Found Animals Foundation

- Finding those specific sources for the story who can provide the answers you need.
- Working out when and where to meet those sources.
- Conceptualizing a mix of open- and closed-ended questions to get the information you need.
- Asking questions in a way that they can get the facts you need and result in at least some good, usable quotes.
- Getting information down quickly and accurately.
- Selecting which facts and quotes best present information your reader needs.
- Putting those materials together in a logical and narrative order that tells the reader a story.

Sounds simple, right?

Interviews are truthfully anything but simple, as they involve asking questions that reflect the information sought as clearly, yet conversationally, as possible. They require listening to and analyzing answers, while at the same time figuring out what to ask next. Interviewers must be nimble, ready to react in the event an answer results in a change to the direction of the conversation or, more significantly, a new direction for the article being pursued. Interviewers read body language. They read between the lines of what is and is not being said.

It might seem like a narrow focus to craft an entire journalism education book exclusively on interviewing, but the need for such a tome speaks directly to the importance of good, strong interviewing in the journalistic field—and the fact it is often a stumbling block for young journalists.

Much like a house will crumble on a weak foundation, so do articles founder when based off poor interviews. The quality of sources, the depth of the questions, the understanding of the subject, and the ability to transmit that subject information to others are key to successful journalism. And much of them start with the interviews conducted with sources who provide journalism with primary source material.

Just because you can ask a question does not mean you have conducted an interview. Understanding the basics behind what makes a strong interview will get us started.

It's All About the Conversation

I interviewed a World War II vet, Norman, who was 90-plus. He was amazing to talk with and hear his memories. When I left his house, I didn't feel like I checked an assignment off. I genuinely enjoyed his company and hearing his story. You have to enjoy conversing with another person instead of thinking like you are interviewing for a story. Maybe they have stories you didn't even expect. That is the key to making it more of a conversation—realize what you are really doing is meeting and getting to know a new person.

(Brittany Schock, *Richland (Ohio) Source* reporter,
personal interview, 2018)

We have interviews every day. They might start by asking a family member or roommate how their day might unfold. It might continue in class or at a job while you figure out the parameters of an assignment. It might happen in a restaurant when you are trying to figure out what on the menu might be gluten-free. When your doctor asks questions to diagnose a cough that is lingering, she is conducting an interview.

Not every encounter, however, is as fruitful as it could be, and we have all had moments of miscommunication (at best), or even unintended offense (at worst). A conversation cannot truly be successful unless both parties are engaged and care about what the other says. As Stephen R. Covey said in the book *The 7 Habits of Highly Effective People: Powerful Lessons in Personal Change*, "Most people do not listen with the intent to understand; they listen with the intent to reply" (Covey, 2004). The same is true in journalistic interviewing.

Think about the biggest challenges we face in communicating conversationally. They might include:

- Distractions, like texting while others talk.
- Asking closed-ended questions that require only one-word response.
- Talking about what we know instead of finding out what others know.
- Asking questions because we feel we have to, without truthfully caring about the answer.

The same issues run parallel in journalism. Distracted communication comes from scribbling instead of making eye contact, and worrying so much about what question comes next that you fail to hear what your source is saying about the current question. We pretend we understand when we really don't, because we fear looking stupid. We ask questions without truthfully caring about the answer.

In this book we are going to break down journalistic interviewing step by step from the beginning, and build through the various environments in which journalists will find themselves interviewing subjects.

Interviewing Basics

> Be prepared but don't be so rigid. Don't have a list of questions that you makes you feel—and your subject feel—like you're going down a checklist. I try to make it a conversation, and try to make it a conversation between equals as much as possible. The person is good at what they do, and that's probably why you're interviewing them.
>
> (Charles Leerhsen, editor and author, personal interview, 2014)

There are five key areas we will focus on as the building blocks of interviewing:

- **Research**: At a cocktail party, it may be OK to start a conversation without having any background information at all, but not so in interviewing. The basics of interviewing start long before a single question is asked, for in journalism there can indeed be stupid questions. For the most part, they are born from a lack of preparation. Familiarizing yourself with as much background on a topic or subject as you reasonably can will bring you to an interview from a position of strength.
- **Sources**: Anyone can answer a question, but how do you find the right person to answer the questions you need answers? First, have an idea what you need to know. Next, figure out who can provide that information. Finally, develop a relationship with the person that will allow them to share that information with you.
- **Questions and answers**: You have done your research and have the perfect source, but now you need to ask questions that are relevant to the source and the topic, and to entice that source to share with you what they know. In some cases, it's more than what they know—it's what they feel or believe or analyze. You must get them to share in ways that provide facts, quotes and anecdotes.
- **Getting it down**: Complex research, perfect sources, insightful questions and great quotes—but did you capture them accurately? That could be the rub! Getting quotes and facts down accurately is a key part of any interview, and it is far more difficult than imagined. For quotes to be quotes, they must be verbatim. But sources talk fast and

their answers can ramble. They may say something as a fact that isn't factual at all. Learning to take notes and factually capture what is said is a primary interview skill.

- **Right questions, right people:** New reporters always ask, "Should I interview a student for this?" or "Should I call the university president's office about this?" It is impossible to answer without knowing what your story is about and what information you need that source to provide to help reader understanding of that story topic. If your story is about why the university decided to raise tuition, there is no real need to interview students. If your story is about how people most affected feel about a proposed tuition hike, then you absolutely need to talk to students.

Most people can learn how to write an article in given style—from news to features, investigations and immersion. But too often the foundation of those articles is weak. The reasons:

- We don't research subjects well enough to fully understand them.
- We don't ask the right questions or dig deep enough with the people who know these subjects the best.
- We don't let people talk and share to the depth needed to help the readers fully engage with the information that frames news.

That is the goal of this book. We will focus on the interwoven elements of journalistic interview, as well as the environments in which interviewing is even more specialized. Remember, no matter what your subject, dig deep, be complete, be fair and make sure every answer you seek advances the readers understanding.

And always get the name of the dog.

Reference

Covey, S. R. (2004). *The 7 Habits of Highly Effective People: Powerful Lessons in Personal Change.* New York: Free Press.

1 Success Starts with Research

I often read this quote from the Bhagavad Gita to my journalism students about cultivating a beginner's mind. It's about a student going to a teacher saying, "I want you to teach me everything you know. I want to sit at your feet and learn from you. So here I am. Teach me." The teacher just starts pouring a cup of tea. And keeps pouring and pouring. The tea is overflowing out of the cup, and the teacher keeps pouring. The student says, "Why are you pouring the tea so it's overflowing onto the floor?" and the teacher says, "This cup of tea is like your mind. It's overflowing with what you already think. There's no room for me to teach you, because it's already full of your own ideas."

(Sarah Saffian, author and writing coach, personal interview, 2014)

How much research is enough before you start interviewing? Enough so that you have all of the answers you need for an intelligent conversation.

"There's some level of information that you do need to have and that you should have otherwise you look like you don't know what you're talking about," says award-winning journalist and author Mac McClelland:

I've been talking to someone, and I realized sort of mid-interview, it wasn't my job to become a Ph.D. on this subject before we had this conversation, but there was definitely a minimum level of information and understanding that I should have had about what we were talking about before I went into it.

Because I didn't have that, I didn't use my time as well as I could have. I wasn't asking as smart of questions as I would have come up with this if I knew what . . . I was talking about.

(Mac McClelland, personal interview, 2014)

Before embarking on a journalistic interview, some basic questions should be asked and answered by you as the reporter:

- What exactly is the story about?
- How many angles are there?

Figure 1.1 Learning to capture notes accurately and completely is one of the most challenging aspects of reporting.
Source: Creative Commons/Jacinta Quesada/FEMA

- Which angle is the one to pursue now?
- Which type of sources would be best?
- What person or organization will be the best source, and how will you get in touch with them?
- What will you ask them?

The more you know, the more likely you are to determine what the reader needs to know. Research comes in all different forms—from relatively pedantic to cutting edge.

In the Beginning

The question asked by most new reporters is, "Where do I start?" As simplistic as it sounds, a straight Google search can be the best place to launch research on a story subject or a source. It can provide background information, previous

Figure 1.2 Searching the web for story ideas and sources has become common practice in journalistic reporting.

Source: Creative Commons

articles, and other support documents and websites. Try filtering by date and looking at the news tab to vary your search and focus on what information you are actually seeking.

Let's consider the story idea of a new bike polo club forming in your neighborhood. Before you even begin to report, it would be useful to look up what exactly is bike polo, how is it played and what are the rules? Go to the news tab on Google and see if anything has been written recently so you might identify some potential sources. Visit YouTube to check out videos of people playing bike polo so you can envision how the sport works. Search on Facebook for people in your area who play bike polo.

The goal of this research is not to become an expert in the subject but rather to put yourself in the mind of the reader. What is it exactly they would want to know, and how can you (a) find sources experienced in this subject to (b) share their knowledge in a way that you can convey the subject meaningfully to the reader?

But to converse with an expert on a topic—from cancer research to a participant in an obscure sport—it is imperative reporters have a base level of understanding, so they can converse meaningfully. The fastest way to turn off an interview subject is by approaching them from a position of weakness—you have no idea what they do or what you need them to provide for the story.

Good reporters live by the adage, "I don't know what I don't know." That means approaching every story and every interview like you know virtually nothing about it. But the last thing you want to do is go into your interview in that state. Building knowledge from the ground up by reading prior articles and documents, asking questions of sources you may not even use, and flushing out as much background as you can will help shape a meaningful conversation/interview with sources.

Despite what your mom or elementary school teacher told you, there are, indeed, stupid questions—specifically ones with which you should have come armed with information, like:

- What is your name and your job?
- What is background relevant to this subject?
- Why are you relevant for my article?

Imagine you are writing a piece on a new company and your first question to the CEO is, "What exactly is it this company does?" How do you think he or she will perceive you from that moment forward?

Your research should provide you with this basic information on an interview subject, as it is often readily available in the public sphere or can be obtained from other sources before you start. You may still want to confirm the information to make sure the source you have is correct.

"I see you grew up in Philadelphia," means you did your research, but they might actually say, "I'm actually from a suburb called Abington." You get

Figure 1.3 Scott Simon said research is important before forming questions, so a reporter knows what he or she wants to talk about under the interview circumstances.

Source: Creative Commons/Tracie Hall

credit for knowing the key info, but you have fine-tuned your facts even further.

NPR's Scott Simon talked research with "Y-Press," a student-run journalism program out of Indianapolis, as part of its "Power-Of-The-Question Project." He said research is important before forming questions, so a reporter knows what he or she wants to talk about under the interview circumstances. He urged interviewers to have a level of expertise, but not to get locked into a strict script:

> I would have to ask myself, "Why are we talking to this person, what do we want to know from them or about from them." At the same time, you have to be responsive to what they say. There is nothing wrong with having a few questions in your mind, but you can't become so devoted to them that you don't notice what someone is saying. Somebody is saying something so you have to listen, and you have to have enough knowledge to follow up on something they say.
>
> (Y-Press, 2009)

The art, according to author and writing coach Sarah Saffian, is to find the balance between being prepared and being flexible. She also cautioned against having so much information that you pre-judge your subject enough to skew your interview:

> As much as I advocate doing the homework, and knowing about the person, and knowing about the context where the person resides, you are really trying to avoid prejudgment as much as possible. That can

---

Box 1.1 How Much Reporting Is Enough?

Charlie Leerhsen, a former editor at *Sports Illustrated* and *People*, and author of *Ty Cobb: A Terrible Beauty*, says he answers the question "How much reporting is enough?" with a simple response: "Too much is enough." Leerhsen says the reason to do thorough research is not just for the data and the facts that it yields, but most importantly to make you confident that you can talk about your subject.

"Ian McEwan, the great novelist, said as a nonfiction writer you want to do enough reporting so you can really walk around inside a subject," Leerhsen says. "You want to do enough reporting so you can really feel confident to put out the story that that you've learned through your reporting. Without enough, you're handing out scraps and bits, and you don't feel confident yourself."

Source: Charlie Leerhsen, personal interview, 2014

really dictate the interview so much that you come home and you don't have any fresh information. You didn't actually gather information, which is supposed to be the point of any reporting.

If you go in there with all the answers what are you going to learn?

(Sarah Saffian, personal interview, 2014)

The Angle

There are often multiple ways to tell a story, and each one is an "angle." It is the direction an article will take, the perspective it will provide the reader, and how the author will shape what the information is provided in the story, via the facts and sources utilized.

To determine the angle, the journalist needs to consider what they want or need the reader to know. It's the lens through which a writer filters information he or she has gathered, and there may be several different angles to pursue from a single news event or feature article.

Consider a news article about a new hospital expansion being built, which results in the closing of a highway off ramp that serves a community. A story could be written about the hospital expansion itself and what it will offer the community. An article could also be written about the impact on the neighborhood of the ramp closing. Two angles to the same story, and each one requires very different sources answering very different questions.

Valentine's Day needs to be covered by most news publications in some way every year, with a unique angle. That angle might be how to spend Valentine's Day as a single person, or finding a couple married 70 years who still celebrate Valentine's Day. It could be visiting a chocolate factory to see how holiday confections are made or spending a day at a winery that makes custom blends and labels for those in love.

Each one is a different angle. Each one would be researched differently. Each one requires different sources.

The research into a story might also allow for the localization of national stories. Consider covering the September 11 anniversary by profiling someone from your community who survived the terror attacks. You could also find in your community transplants from Philadelphia who share how they celebrated the Philadelphia Eagles Super Bowl win.

Search with Social Media

Among the most expansive sources for research is the one used most often for online interaction—social media. The reason: That is where people are.

Facebook has nearly two billion users, while Twitter has more than 300 million. YouTube has 1.5 billion logged-in monthly users. Add in Instagram, Snapchat and countless others, and you can see the access social media provides to people in the world.

Figure 1.4 Social media provides access to sources we might previously not been able to engage—but sites should be used to connect with sources, not conduct interviews.

Source: Creative Commons

Looking for moms whose babies haven't yet slept through the night? Ask on Facebook, check a Twitter hashtag, or seek out an online support group. Trying to find an employee of Apple? Sign into LinkedIn, look up "people who work for Apple" and see if you can connect with them or others who know them.

You can search Facebook, LinkedIn and Twitter for sources in ways that go far beyond finding an individual. Group pages, communities and hashtags can help you network with numerous people who have a similar interest or view.

Join Facebook groups and fan pages of organizations you cover to get insider information on the group and access to members to contact as sources. By going through the "Advance Search" feature on LinkedIn, you can find connections who have a particular interest, employer or skill that might help with an article.

Wonder how to reach that band or celebrity you want to profile? It used to be that an agent was your only real option. Now, hop on Twitter and see if you can get them to respond to a message.

The same applies (to an even greater degree) for seeking witnesses to or participants in, events, sources who live in a certain area, etc. Many are on Twitter and Instagram, and you can search and find them through advanced search or hashtag searches. And third-party apps will allow geolocation of social media users "talking" about specific topics or in proximity to events.

To get started, follow people relevant to your articles or your beat, including government officials, official celebrity accounts, other reporters who cover your same beat, and everyday people in your community who are relevant to specific topics. Following people significant to your work, and engaging with posts that are significant to them, will help you build networks and credibility.

Engaging with hashtags takes the flowing river of Twitter down to a tributary. You can also find story ideas by checking out what hashtags are trending in your community, and find sources engaging on that topic.

Box 1.2 Hi Columbus—It's Me, Summer

Summer Cartwright was an intern at the *Columbus Dispatch* when she set out to do a story about Instagram food accounts. She could have looked them up on Instagram herself, but figured she would only find what she knew to look for, so she spread her call into the world on social media. Her first post was to Twitter:

Hi Columbus. It's me, Summer. What are your favorite local foodie instagrams? Don't have one? Rt this, because I'm sure someone else does. Why should you take this instruction seriously? Because your fav could be featured in the @Dispatch-Alerts & I hear that's pretty cool.

She concurrently put the same post on her Facebook account and, since she was in Columbus, she narrowed that to only reach her friends (or followers) who were in the Ohio's capital city. A direct message approach would work similarly. She added Instagram, and sent out via her personal pages, as well as the newspaper's pages.

"I decided to reach out online because, well, it was an article about social media and the people with the knowledge I was seeking were going to be on social media," she stated in an email. She continued:

I got many responses through my queries. On my personal Facebook I had friends and colleagues comment and even tag accounts with users I would interview. On the company's Instagram I posted a photo and made a story asking for responses and received more than 200 comments tagging pages I should feature. On my personal Instagram I made a story of a screenshot of my tweet. I had friends direct messaging me with account names, and had friends screenshot my story and post it to their page. Twitter was the least successful, but I still received a few mentions that helped in my hunt.

Similarly, I was working on a project on the "professionalization" of youth sports and was seeking a coach working at IMG Academy in Florida, a football-focused private high school. A search on LinkedIn revealed former Ohio State player Jeff Greene was a wide receivers coach there. Now, I did not know Jeff, but he was on Twitter @JGreene_8, so I followed him sent and sent a message:

> @JGreene_8 Hi! I am an Ohio State prof seeking to talk with a coach from IMG Academy. Could we DM?

That led Jeff to follow me back, allowing us to direct message and connect.

Figure 1.5 Summer Cartwright says social media is one of her go-to ways to find sources.

Source: Adam Cairns

Source: Summer Cartwright, email interview, 2018

Asking people for interviews on social media is a little different than asking someone face to face. You lack human connection, and if you are using an @ message (public) instead of a direct message (private), it is open for the world to see. But such a public ask can have far greater reach and may potentially find sources you were not aware of, through people viewing your feed or, if you are lucky, a forward from the source you find.

In truth, people often would like to speak to journalists about topics near to their hearts. They just don't know that journalists are looking for them. Social media lets them come to you.

But remember that media is filled with people who are not who or what they seem. Even if you set up an interview, make sure you confirm the person and their qualifications for your article.

Reference

Y-Press. (2009). Research: Scott Simon part 2. November 21. Retrieved June 20, 2018, from https://vimeo.com/7740942.

2 Something about Sources

It's the beginning of the school year, and a prominent college has changed the way it matches roommates. That news has been reported, but now the student newspaper wants to do a follow-up feature to illustrate some of the biggest challenges of getting matched with an incompatible roommate. What does a young reporter do first?

a. Head to campus and interview students about their roommate experiences.
b. Read a book about the psychology of roommates.
c. Call the school's housing office to determine how roommate pairings have been done in the past, what exactly has changed and why, and conceptualize what exactly you want the reader to know about this topic.

I hope answer C was your answer, as it reflects the guiding principle for every writer: What does the reader want to know? The goal for every article is to think about the questions readers have and for you to get the answers for them before they ever think to ask. To do that, you must find the right sources for each article.

Sources are the keystone of any journalistic project, for without them we have stagnant facts and none of the quotes we need for context and color. Finding sources is like fitting a key and lock—you must have the right key to unlock the right information. Just because you have a person in front of you who has proximity and even relevance to your story, does not make them the ideal source.

Let's go back to the roommate policy story. As a writer I must anticipate readers' questions and what they would wish to know after they were done reading the story. That might include:

1 What was the old policy?
2 What made the school decide to change?
3 What were problems that arose under the old policy?
4 I love to read about other people's misery—can we get some specific examples (anecdotes)?

Figure 2.1 WRAL-TV reporter Adam Owens in Chapel Hill, North Carolina, well demonstrates broadcast reporting technique.

Source: Creative Commons/Caroline Culler

5 I can tell from these examples that a lot of students were dissatisfied, but did anyone have a good experience?

6 How will the school determine if this new policy works?

When we look at the story this way, we start to see exactly what kinds of sources we need, and what kinds of questions we might want to ask.

For the first three, we need a school official who was involved in the old system, the complaints and the change. We can start with the communications office to find them, or we can call student housing and ask who might be able to talk with us. They, of course, will give the "official" school view, and there is sure more to the story.

That means we need students who can also speak on question 3, as well as 4 and 5. But we do not need just any students. It needs to be a student who had a problem with his or her roommate. Just like court, we don't want hearsay evidence ("This happened to a friend of mine") or a fabricated story ("Imagine you are placed with a bad roommate . . ."). We need to get a real person in real time. That means we walk up to a student and ask a prescreening question. You could start with, "Can I ask you some questions about the new roommate policy?"

If that student says, "Yes," and you continue with "What do you think of the new policy?" you might get this response:

"I think it's a good idea. I live off campus with my sister, so I didn't have any problems, but I think it was a good idea to make the change so other people don't have problems."

There are only two options with this quote—and both are a problem for you:

1   You don't use it since it does not answer any of the readers' questions, and you wasted your time.
2   You use it and waste the readers' time, since it doesn't advance the readers' understanding or insights of the topic.

A shocking number of beginning writers pick option 2, thinking a source is a source. But if sources don't help readers, they are useless.

To further narrow, you could ask a source, "Do you live on campus?" or "Do you live with a roommate?," but neither gets to the person you really need. If they live on campus it could be alone, or they could have picked a roommate instead of having one assigned.

Box 2.1 When Less Is More

Charles Leerhsen says not to get discouraged if you don't get the person who's the center of the story as a source, because sometimes that's the last person you want. He cited the example of *Frank Sinatra Has a Cold* by Gay Talese, a legendary profile on the legendary singer, in which Sinatra's voice is never heard.

"Had Frank Sinatra actually shown up in that story and actually had said normal Frank Sinatra things, it wouldn't be as great a story," Leerhsen says. "It would not have the tension of not having him there."

Leerhsen recalls writing a story about Rodney Dangerfield, and the comedian refused to be interviewed. Leerhsen ended up interviewing so many different people around him out of fear of not being able to pull off the story that he got a much better story than if Rodney Dangerfield was interviewed:

> The worst thing for me would have been if he would have finally changed his mind at the end and agreed to be talked to, because then he would have just made it a more of an average normal piece. I think it was a better piece than that.
>
> I often think that Gay Talese left Frank Sinatra out of the piece on purpose . . . because he saw it would be a better piece, and a more tense and dramatic piece without Frank Sinatra's voice in it.
>
> Source: Charles Leerhsen, personal interview, 2014

Consider what you really want to know. Your interview might get off to the best start with, "I'm working on a story about the university's new way of assigning roommates. Did you have a roommate assigned?" A "yes" answer allows you to dig deeper into what they thought about the old policy, how it worked for them, and what they think about the changes. A "no" answer allows you to ask, "Do you know anyone who did?" The more focused you can be in finding your source, the less time you are likely to waste on the sources that don't advance your story.

If it's a profile, the main interview subject is often easy—the person being profiled. But no story is written with one source, and the question often arises: Who do you interview as supporting sources? Once again, the key is answers—who has the information to answer the questions readers will have when they enter the story or project.

Box 2.2 The Police Chase

A police chase with a murder suspect at 5:30 a.m. ends in a residential neighborhood, where the suspect and police exchange more than 100 rounds of gunfire.

The suspect and his girlfriend are killed. Two officers were injured by glass that had been shot out. A stray bullet shot out the window of a nearby coffee shop.

Police hold a press conference to explain the sequence of events, which were the suspects, and the status of the officers. This is an environmental source, as would be your own observations of the scene and the experience. But you also have to think about what else would readers want to know, and who could provide that information?

If I were a reader, I would want to know:

- What it was like for the people in the neighborhood, and anyone in the restaurant?
- What did they hear?
- What were their thoughts?

That means interviewing a personal source—a resident. Make sure to go beyond the "official voice" and get the sources the reader needs.

Source Types

There are numerous types of sources you can utilize for your articles, and here are some of the most common.

Stored: Information Found in a Book or on the Web

It may sound antiquated, but books are still an amazing repository for information and can provide core knowledge that will help you understand a topic more clearly. Before interviewing an astronomer, seek out a book (or chapter) on astronomy; if you want to understand iTunes fully before interviewing an Apple source, reading that chapter in Walter Isaacson's book Steve Jobs will provide insight not likely to be found online.

Websites material is often more current, because it can be readily updated. But there are also numerous sites created with less than credible information, so it's important to seek one that has some evidence of quality. Anyone can create a professional-looking website in a matter of minutes (OK, maybe an hour) so gleaning the "truth" from the web is not as easy as it might appear on first click. Due to the number of links and other search-engine optimized features, Wikipedia is nearly always at the top of search results, and though it has improved in quality, it is still user-generated content. It is better to seek out the original source material listed at the end of each entry.

Working on a story about the health benefits or detriment of coffee? The Center for Disease Control or a story in the *New York Times* might provide usable background information. Data off the site coffeecausescancer.net? Maybe not so much.

Remember also that your original reporting trumps that done by others, so as easy as it might be to cite a website as a source, take the time to actually contact the CDC for a quote as opposed to grabbing info on a web page.

	1	2	3	4	5	6	7	
Name	**Sex**	**Fold**	**Pulse**	**Age**	**Clap**	**Exer**	**Smoke**	**h**
Label								
Type	Factor	Factor	Number	Number	Factor	Factor	Factor	N
Format								
Levels	Female#...	L on R#,...			Left#,#...	Freq#,#...	Heavy#,...	
1	Female	R on L	92	18.25	Left	Some	Never	
2	Male	R on L	104	17.583	Left	None	Regul	
3	Male	L on R	87	16.917	Neither	None	Occas	
4	Male	R on L		20.333	Neither	None	Never	
5	Male	Neither	35	23.667	Right	Some	Never	
6	Female	L on R	64	21	Right	Some	Never	
7	Male	L on R	83	18.833	Right	Freq	Never	
8	Female	R on L	74	35.833	Right	Freq	Never	
9	Male	R on L	72	19	Right	Some	Never	
10	Male	R on L	90	22.333	Right	Some	Never	

Figure 2.2 Data sets contain information that can be analyzed into story ideas and facts for articles.

Source: Creative Commons

Data: Facts and Statistics Collected Together for Reference or Analysis

Think schools in your area are getting better, or worse? Anecdotal evidence of parents whose daughter is in a gifted program and excelling might say they are better. A parent whose son or daughter failed a class might say they are worse. Instead, check out school report cards and standardized test scores from the Department of Education. Wonder if home invasions are really increasing in your coverage area? Check police statistics and the FBI database. Curious how many babies were born nine months after Valentine's Day, contact the Bureau of Vital Statistics.

Online resources have made these searches easier than ever, and research material can be as readily available as typing a word or phrase into a search engine. But remember, not all search returns should be treated equally, and it will take some deeper digging to get to the quality and information you need.

Environmental: What You See and Experience

Being there provides personal experience that can be cited and quoted—and provide contextual descriptions that can go far beyond conventional ideas of sourcing. This involves the color you might get from a crime scene, the dialogue you may recount from a public interaction, or even material being delivered to you, like in a city council meeting, press conference, speech or court proceedings.

In these scenarios, the main goal is to recognize what the main speaker does not provide, and whom you need to find and speak with to get that information.

Personal: Information that You Get from Talking to Real People

This is the best part of being a reporter—being able to talk to real people in real time and getting people to talk to you. This skill is also imperative—and it does not mean sending someone an email, text message or tweet, and awaiting his or her packaged response.

There are certainly challenges. It is scary to talk to strangers, and most newbies to this process feel like they will look or sound stupid and be judged thusly. The only way to get better talking to people is to talk to people. You may feel stupid, but having done good research, determined what questions you need for the reader, and focusing clearly on the right source, you will be ready to start talking intelligently.

Some people are reluctant to talk with reporters. They, too, fear sounding stupid, and they fear being misquoted, taken out of context, or simply being accountable for what they say.

As Collin Binkley of the Associated Press advises:

> A lot of times they are much more willing to talk when you make the case for why they might want to talk to you. When you say to people

Figure 2.3 Collin Binkley says sources are often more willing to talk when reporters explain the need for an interview.

Source: Collin Binkley

you know you guys have a hard job, but people don't get to see how and exactly what they deal with. Sometimes they are more willing to open up when they understand you are coming from that perspective, and you are not just trying to attack them.

(Collin Binkley, personal interview, 2014)

Sometimes people who do want to talk don't have the information you need, or they may have a specific agenda. In the former case, thank them and extract yourself from that interview as smoothly and quickly as possible, and for the latter make sure you reflect fairly and accurately the position from which their comments came, and get another source to balance.

Categories of Personal Sources

Under personal sources, we can put two main categories:

- **Primary sources**: These are the people to whom you absolutely need to talk to get your story completed. Think of these examples:

- Subject of a profile.
- Owner of a new business you wish to feature.
- Police spokesman after a crime.
- City councilman who pushed for a new law.

It can also be a specific category of person, not just an individual. An article about the roommate from hell requires someone who had a roommate from hell, not just someone who had a roommate or, worse yet, never had one. All these sources are imperative to the story, and it would be almost impossible to write without them.

- **Secondary sources**: These are people it is helpful to interview, but maybe not imperative, or there may be a few people who can fit what you need. If you are doing a story on a new restaurant in town, it would be useful to have someone who ate there to comment, but it is not imperative, and there (hopefully) a lot of sources who could fill that role for you.

Box 2.3 Second-Grade Source

I wrote an article on Ohio State astronomy Prof. Scott Gaudi, who received a $750,000 career grant from the National Science Foundation and planned to use some of it to develop science programming of LGBTQ youth. I asked him for some supporting sources, and he gave me coworkers, fellow astronomers and students. They were all important, but one of best anecdotes he gave me about the development of his own science passion revolved around his second-grade teacher, Eleanor Gregory. It was she who had first inspired him to study planets and gave Gaudi a book called "Our Universe." I knew I had questions about his launch into planetary research that only his teacher could answer.

Gaudi provided the name of the school, but when I called there the receptionist said the teacher had retired. I asked them to reach out to her with my name and number, and the reason for my call. Within the hour my phone rang, and Gregory was on the phone. She recalled, "a slightly built boy with caramel-colored hair who constantly peppered her with questions, and pushed teachers and students past their comfort zones, always asking 'why' and 'how,' instead of simply completing assignments as instructed."

Here is a quote I used in the article:

"He annoyed some of the teachers—but not me," she says, adding Scott didn't connect with the playground-going boys in

> class. "He was more interested in thinking about ideas. Not
> everyone at that level felt that was an important part of life."
> Source: Eleanor Gregory, personal interview, 2015

Sources have varying levels of interest and experience in being interviewed, and that will impact how you may interact with them.

Secondary sources fall into several categories. They often have varying
levels of interest and experience in being interviewed, and that will impact
how you may interact with them:

- **Newsmaker seeking coverage:** Leader of a protest movement,
  coordinator of charitable run, owner of new business. These people
  want publicity and are more likely to work with you when it comes
  to setting up and taking time for interviews. They have a clear agenda
  that you need to recognize and adapt your questions to get the
  information you need within their bias.
- **Newsmaker obligated for coverage:** Elected official, entertainer,
  sports figure. These people recognize the need for coverage, but
  are well enough versed to control both their time and their
  message. Those most versed in media have been taught to answer
  the questions they wish they had been asked, not the question you
  may actually be asking. Depending on their level of success, they
  may come with a "handler" like a PR agent, who will intervene
  on tough questions, make sure time limits are held, etc. You need
  to work different angles with your questions to get answers and
  recognize the possibility of manipulation at work.
- **Unintentional newsmaker:** Crime victim, crime witness, lottery
  jackpot winner. These people may or may not want to talk—and
  you can't really force them. What you can do is empathize and
  make sure to acknowledge them as a person in a challenging or
  exciting circumstance. Treat them fairly, as they are not media savvy
  and at moments of high emotion, people are not always clear on
  what they are being asked or what they are saying. Some people
  shut down. Others may rise to the challenge. Take the example of
  Charles Ramsey, a dishwasher from Cleveland hailed as a hero for
  helping to free three women who had been held captive by their
  neighbor Ariel Castro for 10 years: "I heard screaming," Ramsey
  told WEWS-TV in May 2013. "I'm eating my McDonald's. I come
  outside. I see this girl going nuts trying to get out of a house"
  (WEWS-TV, 2013). Ramsey was a media sensation for his animated
  interviews and later wrote a book on his involvement, and his life
  before and after the event.

- **Academics and experts:** These are people you may seek out for their expertise or to report on work they are doing that readers would find compelling. Working on a story about a new basketball academy being built in your town, which charges $27,000 a year? You will definitely want to interview the owner and those involved in the sport in your area. But you may also look up research about the high cost of youth sports and interview the person who did the research.
- **Average people:** There are all kinds of reasons to interview people. They are involved in a topic on which you are reporting (Your hockey team made the playoffs for the first time—how do fans feel? iPad vs. other tablets—why buy one over the other?) These sources are also experts—in the area you are asking them to address. They are not tablet experts, but they do have expertise being a real person using a tablet. Just make sure your questions are specifically tied to their areas of expertise.

The best place to find sources, of course, depends on what sources you need, but there are some keys on which to focus:

Figure 2.4 Interviewing in the field allows journalists to gather more than just words—they get sights, sounds and emotions.

Source: Creative Commons/Robert Thivierge

- **You have to talk to real people in real time.** Email and social media are great tools, but they are no substitute for going to people's offices, businesses, meeting places, etc. Getting a call or a visit from a reporter is a whole lot harder to ignore than an email.
- **You will need to stop people on the streets.** A popular, summer farmer's market has banned dogs, and you need to get comments for a story. You can send emails or reach out through social media, but there is a much faster, easier way to get the sources and quotes you need: Go talk to people at the market!

Yes, it can feel ridiculous and intimidating to stop people on the street and ask them for comments regarding a story, but keep in mind two facts:

- Reporters need thick skins.
- Most people like to have their opinions heard.

Remember that sources beget sources. One of the most successful ways to find sources for your stories is to ask the one good source you have, "Who else might be good to interview for this story?"

That does not mean they will always give you the best people, but they will at least get you started, and maybe your second or third source will also send you in a necessary direction.

"When I'm writing a book about Brett Favre, I'm not just calling (teammates like) Aaron Rodgers and Clay Matthews," says author and sports writer Jeff Pearlman. "I'm calling the free agent who was in camp for two weeks at Delaware State. I'm calling the woman who sold him his house. I'm calling the guy who did his lawn" (personal interview, 2017).

Collin Binkley notes you are never going to get your article done without talking to sources:

> A lot of people just walk up and say, "Hi, I'm a reporter, and this is my story." You can do that or ease into it. Take a second and muster yourself up. An introduction is all you need. "Hey sorry to bother you, but I'm a reporter writing a story." Once you grab their attention for a couple of seconds, you know they are either going to walk away and not say anything to you or they will sit there and talk to you for a couple of minutes.
>
> (Collin Binkley, personal interview, 2014)

Whether you are assigned a story or you pitch one to an editor, you need to know exactly what your story is about and what you want the reader to know when they have finished reading. This comes from narrowing your focus based on what is newsworthy at the moment, and how you can tailor that news to the community you serve through subject or sources.

Readers consume information with one primary focus in mind: "How does this impact me?" That means the better your ability to show the

Figure 2.5 A story on Car2Go will likely include sources from inside and outside the company.

Source: Creative Commons/Julian Herzog

reader why this issue, event or person has some impact on them or their community, the more likely they are to read your article.

Working Backwards

Determining the right source does not begin with the article idea, it begins with what the *finished* article looks like. Once you decide what the finished product *should* look like, determine what information is contained within that story. That information has to be provided based on questions that you develop and ask. Finally, imagine who it is you ask those questions of, and you have the appropriate source.

Let's say the carshare service Car2Go has decided to pull its service out of Columbus, Ohio. The information I want the reader to know when they are done reading the story is why did Car2Go decide to leave Columbus, and what will be the effect on residents and the community as a whole.

Let's consider a sampling of questions will we may to ask:

- Why is Car2Go leaving Columbus?
- How was that decision made?
- How long had the service been available?
- What were the usage figures during the time it was in the city?
- What's the future potential for similar services?
- How does the city feel about this move?

- What kind of negotiations went into trying to keep it?
- How useful was this program to the city while it was here?
- What might replace it?
- What kind of challenge might this prevent to city transportation?
- How will this impact life of a commuter who used the service?
- Why do users think the service left and how do they feel about that?
- Describe how you used the service, and its plusses and minuses.

Now let's consider who will be able to provide the answers to these questions:

- Why is Car2Go leaving Columbus?
- How was that decision made?
- How long had the service been available?
- What were the usage figures during the time it was in the city?
- What's the future potential for similar services?

These answers must come from a Car2Go official, so we will need to reach out to the corporate office media relations department and schedule an interview.

- How does the city feel about this move?
- What kind of negotiations went into trying to keep it?
- How useful was this program to the city while it was here?
- What might replace it?
- What kind of challenge might this prevent to city transportation?
- How will this impact life of a commuter who used the service?

These answers must come from someone in the City of Columbus administration who had been working with transportation and brought Car2Go to the area in the first place. A call to the spokesperson for the mayor or city council would also be helpful to get these answers from the administrative perspective.

- Why do users think the service left and how do they feel about that?
- Describe how you used the service, and its plusses and minuses.

This has users written all over it, so a call may go out over social media seeking sources who had used Car2Go.

How Many Sources Are Enough?

The number of sources required for each article really depends on what is the story being written and what information do you need. As a rule, very few (if any) articles are written with one source. We need varying perspectives on an issue, as well as opposing or confirming viewpoints.

Even a profile on a new basketball coach, which might rely heavily on an interview with him or her, will need to get reaction from the athletic director who made the hire, members of previous teams or coaching staffs and maybe relatively objective observers from the league to provide insights.

The most important way to get started is to find one source—the first source. That source will provide key information for some angle of the article and may also be able to drive you toward *other* sources.

Consider the Car2Go story above. Let's say the Columbus administration official is your first source. You might ask who else would be good to talk to, and they may refer you to another department or elected official who was involved in negotiations, or they may say, "You really need to talk to Jane Smith at Car2Go," and provide the number. You can also ask them for contact information of the Car2Go officials, in the event they have a direct contact to share.

Box 2.4 Begin with the Pitch

I came across a newspaper article on a nationwide increase in home births and successfully pitched it to a magazine after research showed home births in my area had an increase higher than the national average.

My understanding of the story begins with the pitch.

It wasn't just about home birth.

It wasn't just about people who have home births.

It wasn't just about people who advocate for home birth.

The story was about why there was an increase in home birth, and what it means to parents, babies and the medical industry. That meant finding moms who had chosen home birth and had a great experience and ones who hated it or had to be rushed to the hospital mid-birth. I had to find moms from all areas of the city and from different socioeconomic backgrounds, so the story was well rounded. It meant talking to midwives about the benefits and doctors who were opposed. It meant talking to the Bureau of Vital Statistics about the quantifiable numbers of home births.

And all of these people had to be local to the city magazine for which I was writing, or they were useless to me, no matter how skilled or loquacious they may be.

The Approach

Approaching a source in person will set the stage for any discussion, even though it may be the hardest part of early interviews. For most people, walking up a stranger is hard enough, let alone having to start grilling them to get information. The key is to approach it as a conversational relationship, but making sure you are clear on your goals, needs and intentions.

In Person

For the live interview, start as you would any conversation by introducing yourself, stating your goal, and being respectful and polite. For example: "Hi, my name is Nicole Kraft and I am a reporter for The Lantern. I am working on a story about the city's project to put rain gardens on neighborhood streets."

Let's break it down:

- **Introduction:** "Hi, my name is Nicole Kraft and I'm with The Lantern". Your name and publication identify you as a person AND a journalist. Just your name, and people may not realize it's an interview. Just the publication, and it's impersonal.
- **State your goal:** "I am working on an article on the city's project to put rain gardens on neighborhood streets." People you approach cold are not comfortable until they know what it is you want. If you hold off letting them know what you need, you increase anxiety for no reason.
- **Be polite:** "Do you have a minute to talk?" You are asking someone to give up something precious—their time. Don't just launch into questions. Indicate you respect their time by putting at least part of the interview on their terms. If they say "no," you don't necessarily have to abandon them. Be a bit more persistent, and still respectful: "I know you are busy, and I really appreciate your help. I promise it will be quick."

After your interview, ask if you might contact them again if you have more questions, and then get contact information—preferably a phone number, but an email, too, if possible. Finally, thank them for their time and assistance, as it is they who have done you the favor of time and insight.

On the Phone

Phone interviews are easier, because you don't have the inherent discomfort of approaching a stranger face-to-face. They are also more challenging as younger reporters may not be as well practiced speaking on the phone as they are using written communication. It's easy to get flustered on the phone, and easier for sources to be abrupt and cut you off. Practice will help.

Phone interviews start much the same as those done in-person, introducing yourself, stating your goal, and being respectful and polite. The most significant issue is the phone may be seen as an interruption—a person at work is, well, working, and mobile phones are used less for calls than a variety of other interactions.

Unlike in-person interviews, phone sources cannot see that you are not writing as fast as they are talking, or they will not read the confusion on your face when their response is in technospeak or you just don't understand them. Asking someone to slow down will take them out of the interview flow, so using a phone recording app will help keep you accurate. Remember, however, the ethical (and often legal) responsibility you have to ask permission to record a phone call. And if the material is not clear, make sure you ask the same follow-up questions to break it apart for the reader as you would an in-person interview.

By Email

We will talk more about email interviewing in Chapter 4, but the main difference in the approach here is to think of email interaction as the precursor to a live interview. In this case our model of introduction, goals and respect would look more like this.

> Good afternoon,
>
> I hope this note finds you well. I am a reporter with The Lantern working on a story about the new meal plan on campus and what it will mean for students. I am hoping to set up a time we might talk in person or on the phone. My deadline is Friday, so I would greatly appreciate meeting by Thursday afternoon. I can be reached via email or by phone at (614) 555-5555. I look forward to speaking with you
>
> > Sincerely,
> > Nicole Kraft

Notice I did not state my name in the body of the email; there is no need since it will be in my signature. I am also not asking questions here, and I don't really want the answers by email. Instead I want the source to know who I am, the goal of my article and the fact that I want to meet with them for an interview face-to-face, by phone or even by video conference (see Chapter 4).

Stating the deadline is also key to help the source know how quickly they need to be responding.

"Be responsible to your sources," says Jo Ingles of Ohio Public Radio:

> When you interview someone, you don't need to be their friends. Be polite, be responsible. Treat people with respect so they want to work with you again. When you do that it helps you develop a rapport, and if something comes up, they will pitch stories to you. The best stories come from knowing people and being around your beat.
>
> > (Jo Ingles, personal interview, 2018)

Box 2.5 Unnamed Sources

Although students often ask if they can use a source without identification (usually when they have forgotten to get a name or didn't get the spelling), but use of an unnamed source is actually done under extraordinary and limited circumstances when the information cannot be provided any other way.

In the words of *New York Times* public editor Liz Spayd:

> Reporters and editors trust such information, sometimes risking their reputation on it. Readers, on the other hand, couldn't be more suspicious—and with reason. The descriptions generally tilt far more toward protecting the sources than giving readers confidence in what they said.
>
> (Spayd, 2017)

Anonymous sources are synonymous with "Deep Throat," the source for Bob Woodward and Carl Bernstein in their investigation of the Nixon administration. But that example is also living proof that very few sources are actually anonymous. While his or her identify may not be revealed to the public beyond general descriptors (a high-ranking White House official, or a person close to the investigation), their identity is known to the reporters and, likely, an editor. We know now Mark Felt of the FBI was Woodward's source, but Woodward knew it all along.

Journalists using unnamed sources usually know the sources well or their credentials are extensively verified. The importance of information, combined with the inability to get it elsewhere from named sources, will contribute to the use of an unnamed source. Reporters must also consider the source's motivation for providing the information. The relations must be built upon trust —the source to be understood and have the story reported with fairness and accuracy, and the journalist trusting the source to tell the truth.

National Public Radio's guidelines, for example, state it will describe in as much detail as it can how the source "knows this information, their motivations (if any) and any other biographical details that will help a listener or reader evaluate the source's credibility" (NPR, n.d.).

In 2016, the *New York Times* was compelled to issue stricter rules about the use of anonymous sources after articles relying on unnamed officials turned out to be wrong. The *Times* stylebook states that anonymity should be, "a last resort, for situations in which the *Times* could not otherwise publish information it considers newsworthy and reliable" (Paquet, Purdy & Corbett, 2016).

References

NPR. (n.d.). NPR Ethics Handbook. Retrieved June 20, 2018, from http://ethics. npr.org/category/a1-accuracy

Paquet, D., Purdy, M., & Corbett, P. (2016). A Note From Dean Baquet, Matt Purdy and Phil Corbett: New Guidelines on Anonymous Sourcing. March 15. Retrieved June 20, 2018, from www.nytco.com/a-note-from-dean-baquet-matt-purdy-and-phil-corbett-new-guidelines-on-anonymous-sourcing.

Spayd, L. (2017). The Risk of Unnamed Sources? Unconvinced Readers. February 18. Retrieved June 20, 2018, from www.nytimes.com/2017/02/18/public-editor/the-risk-of-unnamed-sources-unconvinced-readers.html.

WEWS-TV. (2013). Charles Ramsey Interview, Rescuer of Amanda Berry, Gina DeJesus and Michelle Knight in Cleveland. May 6. Retrieved June 20, 2018, from www.youtube.com/watch?v=axCn04iXkBg.

3 Getting it Down

A student journalist sat at a coffee shop table, ready to interview a barista about balancing a job while in college. He put a notebook on the table, readied his pen, and asked his first question: "So tell me about a normal day in your job here." The source described her day and what it was like to balance her school, and the reporter scribbled furiously to catch every word—not once lifting his head to make eye contact with the source.

See a problem?

The most important—and challenging—aspect of interviewing is getting down the information that you seek through your interviews. But it's not just getting it down—it's getting it accurate, complete and in context.

What Is Accurate?

In most aspects of life, getting the gist of what someone says is good enough. Not so in reporting where getting facts and statements down exactly as they are spoken is not just professional, it's mandatory.

Journalists conducting interviews must ensure the information that they are taking down from sources is what the source said. That includes verifiable facts, like names, places, dates, titles, etc. Just as important is to make sure it the words spoken represent the questions asked and are presented in context to the questions asked and the story as outlined. Accuracy does not mean every single sentence spoken must be taken down word for words, but anything you plan to quote—contain within quote marks—must be chronicled and presented verbatim.

Taking notes in an interview is not the same as transcribing of every single word spoken. But you also can't just jot down a few words and fill in the rest from our memory. Your notes need to reflect the major points of the interview as it was conducted—including the details of scene and mannerisms that might later help you capture the scene and scenario for readers.

Figure 3.1 Interviewers can use computers, mobile devices or notebooks to take down notes. The choice depends on preference and what will make them the most accurate.
Source: Creative Commons/Pxhere

Taking Notes

The three formats for taking down notes are handwriting, audio recording and typing, and each one has plusses and minuses.

Handwriting

Writing in a notepad is a tried and tested way of gathering notes. Some people love pocket-sized reporting notebooks, while others seek stenographer or legal pads. No matter what the size, notebooks have plusses and minuses. For most people, capturing every word verbatim via this technique is impossible. With written notes, the key is to write quotes you plan to use verbatim. For the other information, you will grab key pieces of information, and also chronicle details from the interview and the interview subject.

Handwriting Plusses

• **Simple and quick:** Stick a notepad and pens in your pocket, backpack, purse, and you are ready to report wherever you are and whenever you go.
• **Easy-to-find quotes:** Circle or star the quotes you are going to use, and you can start writing the second you get to a computer, without transcribing anything.

Figure 3.2 Reporters need to be prepared to take notes in any environment and capture facts and quotes accurately.

Source: Creative Commons/U.S. Photographer's Mate 2nd Class Michael R. McCormick

- **Rarely malfunctions:** No moving parts means you won't run out of batteries or have other technological issues.
- **Durability:** Hardcopy notes are easy to store and retain.
- **Flexibility:** You can write more than what is being said to capture environment and details, as well as draw diagrams or jot side notes.

Handwriting Minuses

- **Hard to read:** Most of us can't write fast and legibly at the same time, so you will need to practice writing quickly, or develop a shorthand that you can later understand.
- **Clunky:** It is not an easy skill to write standing up, and writing and making eye contact with sources is tough.
- **Storage:** Where do you keep all these paper notes, since for legal purposes, reporters should hold notes for a year after publication?
- **Missing in action:** If you lose the notebook, you lose the notes.

Tip: If you do take notes, go as quickly as possible after your interview to a computer or iPad and type those notes into a transcript. The faster you do it,

Figure 3.3 Using an iPhone or a digital recorder can help ensure you get source comments down verbatim.

Source: Nicole Kraft

the more legible will be your handwriting to your eye and the more likely you are to remember key facts and quotes and where they occurred in the interview.

Audio Recording

Using a voice recorder is a popular way of taking notes, and it is now almost ridiculously easy to do so with tools like the iPhone and various recording apps. Whether you use a digital recorder or an app, this method, too, can benefit and limit notetaking.

Audio Recording Pluses

- **Accurate:** Joseph Pulitzer once said there were three main tenets of journalism: accuracy, accuracy, accuracy (Woo & Meyer, 2007). Recording allows reporters to get the most accurate quotes possible since you are capturing ever word in a fixed format.
- **Eye contact:** Recording makes an interview more like a conversation, as you can look your source in the eye and focus on them and

what notes to take. In many instances, the recorder may be forgotten, and you can get into the rhythm of two people talking.

- **Flexibility:** Planning to make an audio slideshow or some broadcast piece with your notes? The digital recording can be used in any number of ways.
- **Storage:** You can digitally store, catalogue and archive interviews easily for future use.

Audio Recording Minuses

- **Breakdown:** Electronics fail, batteries die, memory fills. You may think you have the best recording in the world until you get home and discover a malfunction that makes it all moot (and mute).
- **Transcription:** It takes about twice as long to transcribe a recording as it did to record it, which you better give yourself plenty of time. You also usually transcribe a great deal of information you never end up using, which means wasting time you may not have on deadline. Marking time codes is a good way to keep track of the information you know you will need, but it can get cumbersome and is easy to forget to do.
- **Noise:** Chances are you wouldn't even hear the noisy fan above your head or the clanging of dishes in restaurant until you start listening to a tape recording and realize you can't hear any voices over the cacophony. Our ear lets us filter out noise on which we don't wish to focus. Recorders get it all.
- **Discomfort:** Some people simply don't like the idea of having themselves recorded. You must always ask people if they are willing to be recorded, and if they say no, have a backup plan.
- **Legality:** Although it is always ethically important to ask people if they are willing to be recorded (including recording video that captures sound), in 12 states it is also a matter of legality. The Digital Media Law Project reveals that California, Connecticut, Florida, Illinois, Maryland, Massachusetts, Montana, Nevada, New Hampshire, Pennsylvania and Washington require consent from every party in a phone call or conversation before it may be recorded (Digital Media Law Project, 2018).

By the way, it is almost always illegal to record a phone call or private conversation to which you are not a party.

Typing

Typing notes directly into a computer became a popular technique with the rise of laptops, and it offers a lot of reporter advantages—but it can be a barrier to connecting with sources.

The main advantage of typing into an electronic device is speed. You cut out the step of transcribing since you are basically creating that transcription as you go. In addition, many people who grew up with computers find they type much faster than they handwrite, so using the computer allows for more accurate notes without recording.

On the minus side, however: Think it feels impersonal to write into a notebook? Try staring at a computer screen while someone is talking and comingle the clicking of keys into your interview conversation. It's distracting and impersonal.

Tablets

While it's hard to do an interview politely with a laptop barrier between you and your source, the tablet has advantages in that the screen is much smaller and the keyboard much quieter. In addition, there are apps using it for an interview is no more intrusive than a notebook and can actually provide you with the versatility of a computer and recorder.

Using an Apple Pencil or stylus will turn your tablet into a notebook, and apps will allow for typing, handwriting and recording in the same document, as well as the afford the ability to turn handwriting into typed words.

Testing One, Testing Two

Before starting any interviews, make sure to test your equipment.

We would be hard pressed to find a reporter who has not digitally recorded an interview on a recorder and gotten back to find out their device battery died or the recording was blank for some other reason.

In the old days of tape, I did an entire day's worth of recording with dying batteries. It recorded, but everything played back at half speed. It took me four days to transcribe!

Before you leave, check again to make sure you recorded what you needed. If you need to redo, better to catch your source right in front of you!

Attribution: The Soul of Journalism

What citations are to academic writing, attribution is to journalism. This is how we show people, "Yes, I really did talk to some pretty cool and interesting people who had expertise in this subject, and these are the credentials that mean you should believe them."

In journalistic writing, the writer's opinion means very little. What we need is the opinion of the source, and we need to know why their opinion means something to us. Now we need to identify this person in the article as the source of information we receive and why this source has credibility for this story.

Consider a story on an arts festival that is moving locations to a different part of its city. Let's suppose we get quotes from Scott Stevens, executive director of the City Arts Council. It was the council that decided to move the festival. He is 56 years old and originally from Orange, New Jersey. He has a degree in graphic design from the Art Institute of Philadelphia and is the father of two children. His wife, Jenny, is a stay-at-home mom. He came to the City Arts Council six months ago from the Abington Art Center, where he was assistant director.

How much information do we need to put with Stevens' facts and quotes to show his "expertise" for this story? Basically, we need as much as we need to understand his relevance to us. Here is how they might appear in the article:

> Although the City Arts Council considered keeping the festival in Germantown, the space was simply not big enough, council **Executive Vice President Scott Stevens** said.
>
> We simply outgrew our old space," **said Stevens, who joined the council six months ago from the Abington Arts Center, where he was assistant director**. "This is really the best option
> for everyone who wants the festival to succeed."

We need to know why Stevens is significant to the reader, but much of that information was extraneous to our article.

Attribution is also a way for reporters to stay out of trouble.

Think about a story published at nola.com about high school football player Matthew Tarto, who was found dead in his family home. His father's body was also nearby, and it appeared to be a murder-suicide.

Can we print that, based on the information we have?

As reporters, we have no idea what happened, and unless you actually see someone pull the trigger, you better attribute that information to a qualified source. In this case, reporter Michelle Hunter spoke to the sheriff's office and the coroner to get her information, and we know that because of the attribution she provides (which is bolded here):

> Autopsy results confirmed that 16-year-old Matthew Tarto had been dead for several days before his father, Mark Tarto, committed suicide at the River Ridge home the two shared, **according to authorities. Jefferson Parish Sheriff's Office investigators** suspect Matthew Tarto died at his father's hands. "This has all the earmarks of an apparent murder-suicide, and the autopsy supports that finding," **said Col. John Fortunato, spokesman for the Sheriff's Office.**
>
> **Jefferson Parish coroner Gerry Cvitanovich** said it's difficult for investigators to ascertain Matthew Tarto's exact time of death.

Authorities noted that the thermostat in the home was set very low, cooling the house quite a bit.

(Hunter, 2013)

Reporters can't be the source. Our job is to get the source, and then show us why their views are paramount to our understanding of the story. The information we gather through interviews gets utilized in articles in two primary ways: quoting and paraphrasing:

- **Quoting:** Words in the article are used verbatim—unchanged—and are presented in quote marks (" ") with attribution.
- **Paraphrasing:** Taking the context and intent of what a source says, but with the ability to tighten or change it. The words do not appear in quote marks, but they do have attribution. As a general rule, we paraphrase facts and then support them with quotes.

For example, here is a fact (with attribution) paraphrased in a *Columbus Dispatch* article about swimming pools opening for the summer:

Dave Holstein, manager at Dodge Pool on the West Side, says the new opening schedule will help Columbus match other cities.

And it is supported by this quote:

"Most all pools open Memorial Day weekend," Holstein said, also noting that the city can do so now because, "We're better-staffed than we have been since Ohio State is on semesters. We are going to be adequately staffed."

(Jamerson, 2013)

Here is another from the *Santa Rosa Press Democrat*, in a story on a graffiti exhibit taking over vacant Santa Rosa warehouse.
  Paraphrased fact:

Azzuz, 25, is an art student at the California College of the Arts, and hundreds of startling renditions of the human eye are weaved through the walls of his corner space.

Quote to support:

"I just kind of draw off the top of my head," said Azzuz. "I guess the eyes are kind of like the whole 'window to the soul' thing, and I don't mind a little abjection in my work."

(Taylor, 2014)

Note that the attribution in the quote comes after the first sentence. Putting it first stilts the flow of the quote, and putting it after multiple sentences results in the reader wondering too long, "Who is talking exactly?"

Attribute Everything

Putting "said" in your attribution implies that the information was told to you in spoken words—in person or on the phone. If you didn't get it that way, just let the reader know. Written documents are "stated," so details on the mayor's recent arrest might be "stated in a police report," or "stated in a press release." The same is true if information came in an email ("John Smith stated in an email").

Material paraphrased from a previously published report would be cited as "John Smith told *The New York Times* on May 10," although we try to minimize as much as possible using materials obtained by other reporters, but it sometimes can't be helped when it comes to scoops and enterprise pieces.

And remember: If you quote or paraphrase another person's work so much that you make consuming their materials unnecessary, or you do so without attribution, you are committing plagiarism, one of the most grievous ethical violations in journalism.

On and Off the Record

The goal for every interview is to collect materials to use for our articles. But not everything your sources tell you are intended for publication. Most people have all heard the term "off the record," but it may not mean what you think it does, and it's important both you and your sources know the difference.

- **On-the-record:** Identifying yourself as a reporter and asking a subject if you can ask some questions automatically puts your subject "on-the-record." It's the goal of every journalist for every interview, since it means that everything said can be quoted and attributed. It is the way most interviews will be conducted, but certainly not all.
- **Off-the-record:** When sources have information to share, but don't want it published, they can say they are going "off the record." It means, for all intents and purposes, the statement was never made. It should neither be recorded nor written down.

Off-the-record, however, is not retroactive.

If you are in the middle of an interview, and after a particularly juicy quote your source says, "That was off the record," you have every right to tell them you are afraid it was said on the record and you may need to use it. You and your source can further discuss this issue, and you may decide to honor their request if you wish. If you do not and say it stays on the record, your source may decide he or she is done talking, but the information is yours to use should you feel it's necessary.

Here are some other terms to be aware of:

- **Not for attribution:** Information that can be used in an article but not attributed to the source by name is appropriately considered "not for attribution." We usually ID the source in general terms ("an official in city hall").
- **On background:** If we can use the gist of the information without quoting it at all, or can use it to get others to go on the record, we say that information comes "on background."
- **Deep background:** The information can't be included in the article but journalist use it to better understand an issue, or as a guide to other leads or sources.

References

Digital Media Law Project. (2018). Recording Phone Calls and Conversations. Retrieved June 20, 2018, from www.dmlp.org/legal-guide/recording-phone-calls-and-conversations.

Hunter, M. (2013). Dad Stayed in House with Son's Body for Days before Committing Suicide, Coroner Says. May 29. Retrieved June 15, 2018, from www.nola.com/crime/index.ssf/2013/05/autopsy_confirms_john_curtis_f.html

Jamerson, J. (2013). Two City Pools Open Today. May 25. Retrieved June 15, 2018, from www.dispatch.com/content/stories/local/2013/05/25/two-city-pools-open-today.html

Taylor, D. (2014). Graffiti Exhibit Taking over Vacant Santa Rosa Warehouse. June 25. Retrieved June 15, 2018, from www.pressdemocrat.com/news/2226459-181/graffiti-exhibit-taking-over-vacant?gallery=2339853

Woo, W. F., & Meyer, P. (2007). *Letters from the Editor: Lessons on Journalism and Life.* Columbia, MO: University of Missouri Press.

4 Location Matters

Jennifer Smith Richards of the *Chicago Tribune* recalled a story she reported in her first job out of college, following a school administrator dying of AIDS. The administrator opened up his home to Smith and her photographer, and they visited him two or three times a week over several months.

"He would sit in his chair and smoke and talk to us about what it was like to live with AIDS," she says. "He was very open. He showed us all the drugs that he took, and he talked about his life as school administrator."

The more Smith Richards visited her subject in his place of comfort, the more comfortable he became. And one day he invited the reporters upstairs.

"He took us up to his bedroom, and the bedroom was like a sex dungeon," she recalled. "It was that moment I realized I had done a good enough job as a reporter to make someone say, 'It's all out there, I will show you everything'" (Jennifer Smith Richards, personal interview, 2014).

The environment in which you meet subjects is like a silent partner in the interview process—one that can help a subject open up or keep them on their guard.

The most natural places to meet people you barely know may include a coffee shop or restaurant, and they might work for some interviews. Noise and distraction are surely not friends when it comes to interviewing, but environmental context is. Try someone's home or office, or a place that relates to the story.

In a piece on the rebirth of a city's arts festival, I could have met the director in his office or a neutral location, but the context of the event location provided description that brought the story to life:

> The grass is still wet from a recent rain, but Bicentennial Park in early spring is alive with dog walkers and office workers eating lunch on benches. "Hard to Say" by Dan Fogelberg plays over speakers that ring the fountains where children will frolic when the summer

Figure 4.1 Imagine how different this Katie Couric interview with Secretary of Defense Robert M. Gates would have been had it taken place in an office—or over the phone—as opposed to on the ground with him visiting troops in Iraq.
Source: Creative Commons/Master Sgt. Jerry Morrison, U.S. Air Force

temperatures climb. Outside tables at a new restaurant, Milestone 229, are filling on this unseasonable 80-degree afternoon.

Scott Huntley, as he has nearly every day since taking over earlier this year as director of the Columbus Arts Festival, walks the Scioto Mile along Civic Center Drive. He ends up on the Main Street side of the park and, with his suit coat slung over his right shoulder, surveys the landscape.

"Stand right in this place," he says, "and imagine."

(Kraft, 2012a)

One of the keys to good interviewing is to report beyond the answers and record the environment, how your subject moves and dresses, and what do they act like in their "real" world. Write down what appears compelling or unique to that subject. You may use it. You may not. You won't be able to use it if you don't write it down.

A story on Columbus's new chief of police—the first female and one of only two lesbian chiefs in the nation—took place in her office to capture this:

With a firm handshake and a bright smile, Chief Kim Jacobs comes out from behind her desk to welcome a visitor into her spacious office overlooking Columbus from high atop police headquarters on Marconi Boulevard.

She's only been on the job a few weeks, but the space is already her own, with an image of a rose and the word "Passion" framed on the wall, Ohio State mementos on the bookshelf, family pictures on the crafted cherry wood desk and a suit of armor in the far corner, which she proudly shows off as a symbol of her family name: Knight.

(Kraft, 2012b)

It's clear all of these interviews took place in person, and that has long been the gold standard for how to conduct interviews. In-person interviewing allows you to collect environment, mannerisms, interactions with others and build a relationship with your source that will likely lead to a richer interview.

Writer Sarah Saffian says:

If you can interview a subject in his or her home obviously that's ideal because then you can really get a lot of information, not just from what they're saying that's coming out of their mouths, but their national environment. If they interact with a family member or a friend all of that can be good pick up information or just tagging

Figure 4.2 Sarah Saffian said watching a source interact with a family member or a friend can provide good information.

Source: Sarah Saffian

along as they go about their day as opposed to taking them out of their environment and putting them in some neutral place like a publicist office or something that's not going to give you any information about them.

(Sarah Saffian, personal interview, 2014)

When you go out in the world to interview subjects, there is more to consider than just where the interview takes place, as the following sections show.

Be on Time

Are you one of those people who runs five minutes late and thinks it's not a big deal? Those days are over as soon as you decide to be a reporter. Journalists live being on time for deadlines, and there is no space or time for you to be late to meet with interview subjects.

How Firm Thy Handshake

The first step to any good conversation is the introduction, and interviews are no different. Whether you are stopping someone at an auto accident for comment or meeting for a lengthy profile, be sure to start conversationally: "Hi. How are you?" Then introduce yourself and tell your source what publication for which you are writing.

Make eye contact and offer a firm handshake, and have your notebook or recorder ready to go, or easy to access. Fumbling looks—and is—unprofessional.

Dressing Up

It is easy to be so focus on every other aspect of the interview—what are my questions, where do we meet, etc.—that you forget that you never get that second chance to make a first impression.

For live interviewing, that means dressing so that someone feels like you respect yourself as much as you need him or her to respect you. Common classroom dress—sweats, jeans, T-shirts, pajamas, shorts—does not fly in the business world, and it will impact how your interview subject feels about his interviewer.

At the same time, though, we have to make our subjects feel comfortable. That means wearing a dress or suit to meet with a farmer to talk about the impact of ethanol on corn prices can be just as damaging as heading to an interview with a bank manager and wearing jeans and your favorite Ohio State sweatshirt. You have lost respect in the eyes of both.

Even dressing up by your own standards may not be suitable to the standards of others. Like it or not, a lot of skirt styles are pretty short, and tops are pretty low, and both will give an interview subject an impression —just maybe not the one you want.

And your favorite Buckeye jersey? Never appropriate any time but game day (and as a sports writer, even that is not appropriate; see Chapter 7).

So how do you dress? The answer lies in understanding exactly whom you are meeting with and understanding their expectations. Dressing for a media interview is a lot like dressing for a job interview. You want to make the best possible impression without making your subject uncomfortable.

Someone in business or government will treat you with more respect if you dress like him or her—but a step below. A sports coat and tie with khakis, or slacks with a nice blouse would be fine. For someone in agriculture who may be dressed to work with animals or in the field, dress a step up—nice jeans with boots and a button-down shirt may be good, while the sports coat would be a bit too much.

Every aspect of dress—from shirt to shoes, to even the way you take notes can influence an interview subject, according to Charles Leerhsen, who interviewed numerous celebrities in his editor roles at "People" and "Us Weekly".

"You should always dress to show that you're somebody; you're not just a schlub," Leerhsen advises:

> I even take it to the point of trying to have a fancy pen with me if I'm going to use a pen to take notes. The subject may never notice the pen, or may never notice me even, but if she or he is going to notice me I want them to see a person who is a as worthy as they are just in it just on the other side of the fence in another business. Therefore, they'll respect me, and I think they'll give me better information.
>
> (Charles Leerhsen, personal interview, 2014)

Body Language

Remember also, how your body language can impact how a question is perceived. Are your arms crossed? Are you rolling your eyes? Lifting an eyebrow? Sighing during the answer? Trust me—interview subjects are not blind, and they are certainly not dumb or insensitive. Interviewing is all about the golden rule: Treat others as you would wish to be treated yourself.

Next Best Things to Being There

Unfortunately, it's not always reasonable to interview in person. It requires that our interview subject is local or we have the ability to travel to meet in person. It can also be inconvenient for tight-deadline journalists, busy sources

Figure 4.3 The telephone has long been a staple of reporting, as is shown by reporter Bill Wallace of the San Francisco Chronicle in 1994.
Source: Creative Commons/Nancy Wong

and those working on stories far away from their sources. We also have to decide if it's worth setting up a live appointment, driving 20 minutes in each direction and settling in for a 10-minute interview on a topic that could have been done on the phone—in 10 minutes.

That means we have to look at other options.

Phone

Phone is the next best option to being in person and remains a mainstay of many reporters. You can reach people quickly, and it is often more likely a busy source will give you 10 minutes on the phone as opposed to taking even more time for a face-to-face interview. For busy reporters, phone provides the opportunity to connect with a multitude of sources in a much shorter time frame, and the ability to type in notes while talking, so they are ready to be used right away, instead of having to transcribe.

You can also record calls (provided you follow the legal and ethical guidelines we discussed in Chapter 3) with apps such as Tape A Call or Google Voice, which will provide MP3 files of your interview for backup.

In phone interviews, timing may be everything, so think about what might be happening on the other end of the phone before you call. Most people do not have a ton of free time or mental energy in the first hour of their day's work, right before lunch and when they are trying to get work down at the end of the day before going home. That makes the best times to call in the 10–11 a.m. range, and the 2–3:30 p.m. range. Calling people at home means navigating kids and dinner, so early evening might work best—often 7–9 p.m.

And when you make that call, have an idea the name of the person you want to speak with. Asking for the manager or CEO implies to the person answering the phone you may be a telemarketer or you just don't know what you are doing. A scouting call or email, or simple web search, can reveal the exact person you need.

As easy as the phone may be to connect with sources, it has limitations. You cannot judge body language or facial expressions, as you would in an in-person interview, but phone allows live connectivity to sources, the ability to gauge voice tone and tenor, and the opportunity for immediate follow-up questions.

When you call someone—and they answer—introduce yourself and tell them what your story is about and what you are seeking from them. Then ask, "Is this a good time?" Hopefully they will say, "yes," and you are ready to start your interview.

Even if they say "no," don't let them go now that you have them. My standard line is "I only need about two minutes of your time." Most people can spare two minutes—even though my interview may, in reality, take longer (although this tactic won't work if I am sure I need 30 minutes or an hour).

And if they really don't have two minutes, pin them down on another interview time right there and then—and make sure you call them. That way you have greater likelihood that interview will actually take place.

Video

With video conference services like Skype, Zoom, Adobe Connect or FaceTime, set up through email is often the most effective way to agree on a time and share a link to a video conference site or share Skype handles. We have not yet gotten to the *Star Trek* point that cold video calling is acceptable, but it may be coming.

Video will allow you to see more body language, although you are clearly not engaging someone in their natural habitat when they are tethered to a computer or mobile device.

Both phone and video can also be recorded for accuracy and even multimedia purposes, provided you get follow legal (and ethical) recording requirements.

Email

This seems like a great interview option—simply send someone the questions, and they will answer them for you. All you need to do is cut and paste the quotes into your article. You barely have to type anything. You can also reach out to people and let them respond at a time that works for them, which seems like it should make sources happier.

If this sounds too good to be true, it is.

Student-journalists tell me email has become their go-to means of interacting with sources for two primary reasons: a) They worry about bothering people by seeking in-person interviews, and b) in an online world some lack the confidence to ask and answer questions in a face-to face interview. So even though we teach them over and over to avoid email interviews, a few every semester try to sneak one in.

"I think it's a generational thing," says Lane DeGregory, the Pulitzer Prize-winning *Tampa Bay Times* staff writer. "The way they grew up with social media and texting, that's a big part of communication. To sit down and look someone in an eye is more difficult. The art of conversation is not as much a part of their relationship" (personal interview, 2018).

There are, however, significant challenges to email interviews, which should make it a last resort.

- They sound stiff—like they are written and not spoken (because they are!).
- Answers are also crafted and edited, lacking any real candor.
- Follow-up questions lack any spontaneity.
- Giving people ample time to respond may mean they have little sense of deadline or urgency and can leave you hanging.
- An email address is no guarantee that is who is answering your query.

Paul Oren, a radio journalist who now lectures at Valparaiso University, recalls assigning students to write a historical piece on a campus group and telling them to use as sources members from 15 years ago. A week later when he asked how interviews were coming, he was told they had emailed but not heard back, so they were no closer to completion than they had been when assigned.

Students think they have done their job because they put the email out there, but in truth they have no ideas if that email went into the spam folder, got ignored or was ever even received, Oren says:

I strongly advise against email interviews. I think it makes everything easier and interviewing someone shouldn't be easy. Interviews via email eliminate the ability to ask follow up questions as the conversation is happening. The power of observation in an interview is so important. You hope you get people to the point people forget they are being interviewed and have a conversation. That never happens with email.

(Paul Oren, personal interview, 2018)

Oren notes it's impossible to read body language through email, and nuances like humor is often lost. "You want people to tell you the truth," he says. "You don't want a version of the truth put through a filter."

That is not to say journalists don't use email at all. It's a terrific tool to set up an interview—although that request can be ignored as well. It is also useful after an interview to reach back out to a source with follow-up questions. One of the last questions I will ask in an interview is if I can reach out with follow-ups, and what would be the best way to contact the source, and email may be that best option. It's also effective to thank a source after an interview.

In reality, there may also be times when email is the only option provided.

Chris Davey, who was a student journalist and a reporter before becoming vice president of communications for Ohio State University, says he requires many interviews via email. He says in an age when student articles spread far beyond campus borders to a global audience, the need for accuracy trumps any challenges with an email interview:

I need to ensure things are correct, and are not being misunderstood. Not seeing inaccuracy reported is like job No. 1 for me. Dealing with student journalists, [email] helps ensure the highest degree of accuracy. Email is just a delivery method for expressing yourself in the public sphere. Sometimes the back and forth with a reporter by email will become so conversational it starts to function like an interview.

(Chris Davey, 2018)

As much as journalism professors and journalists might wish to avoid email interviews, they are likely going to be mandated at points by sources, and here are some keys to success:

1   Make sure the questions are specific, succinct and answerable: The best email questions most often deal with empirical facts, rather than opinions or characterizations.
2   Plan to paraphrase, not quote, much of the information: It will help with the stilted nature of responses.
3   Don't be afraid of the follow-up question: Be sure to let the source know in the initial interview you will be reaching out again with more question as needed.

Figure 4.4 The email interview may be convenient, but Paul Oren said they rarely serve the interviewer or the reader well.

Source: Paul Oren

4   Read the responses quickly to ensure you have what you need, so you don't keep an email interview going over several days.

5   Always indicate that you have conducted the interview in an email. Remember, "said" means you actually spoke to someone. "Stated in an email," is proper attribution.

Box 4.1 Report, Write, Rewrite

I did a profile on National Hockey League defenseman Jack Johnson when he arrived at the Columbus Blue Jackets. My interview time lasted two hours before I spent another two hours with him at a fan event, including a private meet and greet and a public autograph session. I must have filled 20 pages with notes on people he met (including names, spelling and ages), comments he made, how he looked, what he wore—with no clear idea of how I would use any of it.

My initial lede went like this:

Jack Johnson has every reason to not want to be a Columbus Blue Jacket.

When he came here from the Los Angeles Kings in February of 2012, in a trade for disgruntled Jeff Carter, the team was mired in last place.

Two months after the Jackets ended their season in the NHL cellar, Johnson watched from his home in Michigan while that Kings team—with whom he spent the first six years of his career —won a Stanley Cup championship without him.

And two months before the start of the 2012-2013 season, the Jackets traded away its captain—and best player—Rick Nash.

Jack Johnson could be forgiven for feeling he entered hockey purgatory with his trade to Columbus. Except he doesn't.

"You never want to be part of a last place team, especially as an athlete," Johnson says. "But the opportunity comes along [rarely] in sports where you can be involved in a rebuilding. I know the fans are tired of hearing that, but it's a rare thing in sports to mold a team where you think it should be to win, to start a new culture.

"And that's what we are going to do here."

My editor, however, wanted it to be more personal, and to better "see" Johnson. Thank goodness I had that book filled with notes, or I would have been hyperventilating. I flipped through my notes and came back with this in less than two hours (speedy revisions make editors happy):

The line snakes across the Nationwide Arena main floor like a Disneyland ride, as Jack Johnson strides from beneath the stands on black Nikes. Ice will cover this spot two months from now, but tonight's destination for the newest Blue Jackets star is an 8-foot-long table adorned an array of black, blue and silver Sharpie pens.

Dressed in a blue T-shirt and jeans that do little to hide his linebacker physique, Johnson's hands are tucked shyly in his pockets, his blond hair freshly gelled off his forehead, as he places two bottles of water on the table, takes a seat at the lone folding chair and uncaps a pen.

Johnson then looks up at the first person in line, who waited more than 60 minutes at a pre-season ticket promotion, a smile spreading wide across his face and crinkling his blue eyes with a welcome that feels like solidifying a new friendship.

Fan after fan then comes forward, handing Johnson pucks and pennants, jerseys and flags, trading cards and mini helmets, asking for a photo or, in the case of preteen Maykala Tuttle, a hug.

And Johnson accommodates every one with a smile, sometimes a handshake, his demeanor indicating—true or not—that he has all the time in the world and no place that he would rather be.

Figure 4.5 A profile on NHL star Jack Johnson came to life by following him on various public events.

Source: Nicole Kraft

Note: After the 2012/13 NHL Lockout I ended up having to revise the story again—requiring yet another interview with Johnson. Such is the writing life!

Source: Kraft (2013)

References

Kraft, N. (2012a). Down by the River. May 1. Retrieved June 20, 2018, from www.columbusmonthly.com/content/stories/2012/05/down-by-the-river.html.

Kraft, N. (2012b). The Columbus Way. July 1. Retrieved June 20, 2018, from www.columbusmonthly.com/content/stories/2012/07/the-columbus-way.html.

Kraft, N. (2013). Ice Breaker: Meet Jack Johnson, the Promising Defenseman Who Joined the Blue Jackets Lineup Late Last Season. Does He Have What it Takes to Turn Our Floundering Franchise into an NHL Contender? *Columbus Monthly*, March.

5   Questions and Answers

When LeBron James first came to the Cleveland Cavaliers as a rookie, he declined requests for one-on-one interviews. But Tom Withers of the Associated Press was not going to give up asking for one from the team's media relations department.

"I didn't badger them, but I stayed on top of it and reminded (the team) I'd love the chance to sit down," Withers says.

Finally, Withers got his opportunity at a turkey giveaway at a Baptist church. James was sitting at a table, surrounded by his "posse," and Withers admitted the first few minutes of their dialogue felt forced and uncomfortable. After a few minutes, James dismissed everyone but Withers, and the two began to talk.

> We got into deeper stuff with LeBron talking about his absentee father, the struggles of his mom, and finally I hit a chord with him where it shifted, and he began recalling the difficulty of his childhood. He went back to where he was as a little boy—while he was talking to me.
>
> That became the lede, when he closed his eyes and, for that moment, he was 8 years old again.
>
> (Tom Withers, personal interview, 2018)

Box 5.1 "He Remembers It All"

Here is the lede of Tom Wither's interview with LeBron James, published December 12, 2005:

> For an instant, LeBron James again sees life through the frightened eyes of a fatherless 8-year-old boy.
>
> Sitting in the basement conference room of Antioch Baptist Church, James has just finished handing out Thanksgiving groceries to families as needy as his own once was.
>
> A few weeks shy of his 21st birthday, the Cavaliers' superstar is allowing a rare glimpse into his well-guarded privacy during an

exclusive interview with The Associated Press. He's upbeat while openly discussing fatherhood, wanting to win an NBA championship in Cleveland, his upcoming contract extension, personal goals and dreams—but then a question about his past seems to awaken painful memories.

Leaning back in his chair, a flashback momentarily walks James back in time.

An only child—and not yet a basketball prodigy—James is being raised in Akron by a strong single mother who has nurtured her son with love but little else. She preaches to him to be fiercely independent, respectful and kind. She tells him to fear no one.

Most important, Gloria James teaches young LeBron how to be a man.

Money is tight so the pair move frequently, fleeing tough neighborhoods around the Rubber City where he is exposed to the harsh realities of America's urban decay.

On a chilly November day years later, he remembers it all.

"I've seen a lot of stuff that kids my age just don't see," James says, hinting at a darkness he would prefer stay hidden. "That's where the knowledge comes from. I don't want to go back to what I've seen when I was 7, 8, 9 years old."

Asked for an example, James pauses and shifts in his seat. Staring at the floor, he's unsure how to respond.

Things on the street?

"Everything," he says. "Everything that's not right. I think that's where I got my knowledge."

Source: Withers (2005)

If journalism is all about stories, then interviewing is all about the conversations that lead to those stories. It is no accident that "view" is part of the word "interview." An interviewer's goal is to see in words, facts and information, opinions and quotes.

The most successful print or multimedia interviewers see an interview subject as the most fascinating person they might have met at a cocktail party, but one on which they have conducted extensive research and already know what information they might want to glean from talking with them. Where interviewers fail is they think in terms of questions. We must instead think in terms of answers.

Figure 5.1 Persistence and asking the right questions at the right time helped AP writer Tom
Withers break down LeBron James's defenses and get the interview of a lifetime.
Source: Creative Commons/Keith Allison

It's not a matter of crafting the perfect question and hoping to get the
right answer. Rather, think of what answer you want or need, and then
determine how to ask a question to get that response. Remember to
think like the reader. For most people, the answer to one question leads
to another question, and so on, until their curiosity is satiated. You must
think for readers to answer their questions before they even know
to ask.

John Sawatsky of ESPN, a Canadian author, journalist and interviewing
expert, describes interviews as a function of the questions asked. He told
students at Y-Press, a nonprofit Indiana youth-media organization, that a
bad answer means there is something wrong in the question. In his view
good questions have two components—a topic and a demand. The topic
must be narrow enough to get a good answer (Y-Press, 2009). He cites
these examples:

- "What do you think about the Yankees winning last night?" (Broad)
- "What do you think about the home run hit in the bottom of the seventh inning in the game the Yankees won last night?" (Narrower)

The key to getting good answers is asking the best questions you can in a structure that compels your subject to want to answer as fully and colorfully as possible.

Keep Questions Open-Ended

Question formation 101 revolves around the two major types of questions we can ask:

- Closed-ended
- Open-ended.

Closed-ended questions result in one-word answers, often "yes" or "no." For example:

- "Do you like your job?"
- "Did you enjoy visiting Croatia?"
- "How old are you?"

You need them for some questions that are more fact-based (like the age one), but relying on them too much results in confirmation of facts but no insights or useful quotes.

Open-ended questions let people extrapolate in their answer, and they provide more insights and quotability. A lot of times these questions take the form of:

- "How did you feel ..."
- "What were you thinking when ..."
- "Describe how you ..."

Beware of Leading Questions

You hear these questions in sports all the time: "Coach, don't you think that play in the third quarter showed the power of your offense?" When they say, "Sure," that becomes a fact in your story. Your job is not to tell a source what he or she is thinking, but rather to ask questions that let them contemplate, and formulate thoughts and ideas related to your article topic.

Develop Ideas, Not Questions

Use your list of questions as a guideline, as opposed to a mandate. Few things sound more artificial then reading a question off a piece of paper or an iPad to your subject, and chances are their answers will be just as stiff.

Think about phrasing each question like you are sitting across from an acquaintance or friend at a coffee shop, and use similar phraseology and body language.

Suppose you want to interview a professor about a new major being developed at a college. If you think answers first, you might develop a list like this:

- Where did the idea for the major come?
- How did it get developed?
- What do you hope the major will teach students?
- What kinds of students take the major?
- How many and which classes are part of the major, and why?

Rather than asking question No. 1 verbatim, try, "I was looking through the major, and it seems really interesting. I wondered where the idea came from to put all this together as a major."

"Be prepared, but don't be so rigid," says Charlie Leerhsen. "I try to make it a conversation between equals as much as possible. The person is good at what they do, and that's probably why you're interviewing them —even if they're good at murdering people. And you're good at what you do" (personal interview, 2014).

That being said, as a student, it may be easier to write out your questions at first. You may change your style later.

The choice is yours, but make sure your source is comfortable, and that you listen to ensure you know which question comes next—regardless of what comes next on your list.

Go with the Flow

Deciding the order for your questions is one of the most challenging and important interview skills you can develop. The flow of questions needs to seem natural and conversational. That means recognizing your subject may answer your questions out of order, before you've even had a chance to ask them, or they make take you in different directions than you had intended.

Listen to how the responses are coming in, and see if there is a natural flow at work. Don't just ask question No. 5 because it follows question No. 4. It's possible based on the subject's response that questions No. 10 is a much more logical follow-up, or that you have gone into uncharted territory. And don't be afraid to let your interview go where the interview takes you. You may be pleasantly surprised.

John Sawatsky advocates reporters order questions in the same sequence that people's minds think—start at the beginning and go through the story. Starting at the end can confuse the thinking process.

"People sequence chronologically," he told Ypress students. "Sequence in same order, and they will tell you more. They will build momentum and momentum will carry them, and they will reveal things you don't even know to ask about" (Y-Press, 2009).

Body Language

There are few things more disconcerting then being asked a question, and the interviewer it is slumped in a chair, huddled over a notebook, and doesn't make any eye contact when you are talking. Make eye contact. Lean in as you ask questions so your source recognizes that you are interested in the answer.

Just Ask the Question Already

It is imperative to know what you want to ask, and then just ask it. Some interviewers ramble on so long asking the question, it's a wonder the subject remember the topic.

Author and writing coach Sarah Saffian says:

> I kind of call it the Charlie Rose syndrome where he asks this long, involved question, and he's talking and talking and talking. Basically, the interesting subject he had on his show just says "yea" or "no," and that's the quote. It's one thing if it's broadcast journalism, because you get to see the interchange, but for a print journalist all you've got is this one-word quote and that's not working.
>
> (Sarah Saffian, personal interview, 2014)

Listen

It is easy to ask questions. What is far more difficult is to actually listen to what someone is saying, especially while you are taking notes, jotting down follow up opportunities and trying to think of your next question. It is imperative that you really hear the answers, and let sources talk, without interrupting, until they have finished their thought. Only then will you know where the interview is going next.

Award-winning author Mac McClelland can always tell when an interviewer is just going down his or her questions without really caring about the answer:

You say something and then there's follow-up questions, and you're thinking, 'You are totally not listening to what I'm saying. That's not how I approach conversations with people in normal circumstances, and I assume most people don't either.

If you have the habit of listening to your friends when they're talking to you, it's the same sort of courtesy you should be extending to strangers, to actually listen to them.

(Mac McClelland, personal interview, 2014)

Box 5.2 When "What Was in Your Mind" Goes Wrong

Sometimes even a perfectly fine open-ended question can go awry. Consider this exchange between LeBron James and ESPN's Mark Schwarz on June 6, 2018, a short time after the Cavaliers went down 3-0 to the Golden State Warriors in the NBA Playoffs.

The dialogue came three days after Schwarz tried to get James to express his thoughts on an error by Cavaliers teammate J. R. Smith that cost the team a previous win in Game 1 of the finals:

Schwarz: Describe what was in your mind both tonight and last year when Kevin Durant launched that shot from the wing.

LeBron: I actually think you should be like a psychiatrist. You want to just keep trying to get in somebody's mind? That's your whole thing, huh Mark? What's in my mind? Miss it, so we can get a rebound.

Schwarz: Did it feel like last year to you? Did you think of it in that moment?

LeBron: No.

(Curtis, 2018)

Stories Are Not Boring—Writers Are

Not all stories are sexy or involve celebrity interviews or scandal. Some stories may, on first assignment, appear flat-out boring:

- New sewer lines being put down in your beat—yeah!
- Cat rescue has too many cats—bummer!
- Furniture store celebrates 50th anniversary—yippee!

It is not, however, the story that is boring—it's your attitude or approach toward it.

Start every assignment by thinking what a reader would find interesting, and then, if you must, force yourself to feign interest in that story. That means every interview with a source should appear to be fascinating to you—even though you and I both know it may not be.

Get up close and personal with those sewer lines, literally in the trenches as they are being installed, and write about what you see and hear and smell. Visit the rescue and just watch and listen. What do too many cats sound, smell and feel like? Write it down and show us in words.

A 50th anniversary of that store means someone—or likely some family or partnership—devoted half a century to a single business in a community that has likely come to count on it in some way. What was the neighborhood like 50 years ago? How does someone stay engaged in the same business for 50 years? The sources you are interviewing care about their subject, and just like kids and dogs know when you don't like them, sources know when you don't care about their subject.

One of the best parts of being a reporter is getting to meet people you didn't know who can talk on subjects you may have never considered. Give yourself the opportunity to incorporate the story into your own psyche, at least for the time you are writing it.

How Many Questions Do You Need?

Journalists the world over debate how many questions to bring to an interview—if any. There are those who write questions out—usually between 10 and 20—and those who write out topics to cover.

"Way back when I was on the daily paper at Penn State, I remember our advisor telling us to have no less than 20 questions, no matter how long or short the interview," writer and blogger Sally Kuzemchak says. "I can't say that I do 20 now, but I feel like 10 is a good number. If I need one quote for one graph and I sort of already know the gist of what I want them to say, I could go into that interview with one question, but I try very hard to have a list" (personal interview, 2014).

The Bell Curve

Every interview has questions that are easy to answer ("How long have you been married?"), harder to answer ("Why did you leave the company you founded?") and all kinds of questions in between ("Let's talk about where that idea came from").

The question for you is: In what order do you ask your interview questions?

Remember that this interview is a conversation, so what would happen if you shook hands with a new acquaintance and immediately started talking about their recent divorce, lost job or the fact that neighbors think his or her yard is a dump.

Chances are that conversation won't last long.

The same can apply when you are interviewing a school board candidate who recently learned she was unendorsed by her party for making comments supporting charter schools. When you sit down to interview her, think about how you can lay a path that will take you to the big news but will make her comfortable enough to want to get there with you specifically.

Be sure to start by saying hello and asking how she is, or how her day has been. I don't mean to be patronizing, but many a young reporter is so focused on starting an interview that he or she forgets to be polite.

Then we could try talking about the campaign and how it's going. Commiserate that the end is near and talk about how she is feeling—tired, invigorated, etc. If you know a subject is delicate, acknowledge it: "I know things just got a bit tougher with the unendorsement. Let's talk about that . . ."

The point is, you have made her feel like a person, not just a source. And chances are she will answer you person-to-person, and not with rehearsed answers (at best) or defensive ones (at worst).

Brittany Schock of the *Richland Source* reported a series on infant mortality, which included interviewing women who had lost their babies. She knew the order in which she asked her questions would determine how deep the women would get in talking of their loss:

> You don't start with, "How did you feel when your baby died?" Even before I hit record, we'd talk about life, latest movie they saw. I'd ask them to tell me about their daughter, their other kids, what do they remember about when she was born and the craziness of newborn. Then I ask them to tell me what happened when you lost her. A lot of times they don't even realize they are uncomfortable. They don't realize they are nervous. It's just so natural a conversation.
>
> I work hard for them to trust them and related to me as a human being. My goal was making them comfortable with me as a person before talk about precarious things. And I'd tell them, "Let me know if you need to stop," and tell them I was so thankful for them telling me this story, as it was going to help a lot of people.
>
> (Brittany Schock, personal interview, 2018)

Box 5.3 Carving Out Character in 30 Questions

Lane DeGregory is considered one of journalism's best interviewers, and she offers these questions as a framework to dig deep into a subject's character.

1 Tell me the story of your life . . .
2 What's your earliest memory?

3   Describe your family, house, pets . . . and how you fit into the dynamics . . .

4   Recreate some family traditions, holidays—best and worst . . .

5   What did you want to be? Did you picture yourself married? Children?

6   Were you popular in school . . . what activities did you do?

7   Who were your heroes . . . and why? . . . Who are they now?

8   What was your first experience with death?

9   How did you meet your girlfriend, spouse, best friend?

10   Tell me about the most difficult decision you ever had to make . . .

11   What do you dream about?

12   Who knows you best? Who do you confide in?

13   Do you believe in God? Go to church? What do you pray for?

14   Are you politically involved? How active? Why?

15   What's in your wallet . . . or purse . . . car . . . or Ipod . . . refrigerator?

16   What do you worry about most for yourself? Your family? The world?

17   What do you want most, with what's left of your life?

18   What are you searching for, questions you still have?

19   What do you regret and why?

20   If you could relive any moment, what would it be, would you change it?

21   What one word would best describe you?

22   What do people misunderstand or assume about you?

23   Tell me something about you that few people know . . .

24   What bugs you most about yourself? Others?

25   Do you want your children to be like you when they grow up? Why?

26   What are you most proud of?

27   What do you think happens to us after we die?

28   Why are you here, on this earth, at this time?

29   Who will come to your funeral?

30   What do you want to be remembered for?

Source: Lane DeGregory, email correspondence, May 2, 2018

Surgical Strike

There are, of course, circumstances when the bell curve does not work, such as more pointed interviews.

When you are in the midst of a breaking story, and you need a meeting with the mayor faced with a citywide issue or a superintendent embroiled in controversy, once you say hello, the direct questions begin.

Jennifer Smith Richards was with the *Columbus Dispatch* covering schools when she began to take notice of Champion Middle School in Columbus, Ohio. By examining data, Smith Richards was able to determine that Champion was not just the worst performing school in Columbus—it was actually the worst performing school in Ohio. That led her to some pointed interviews with Columbus City School administrators.

And she never apologized for the questions that she asked related to her story, knowing they were part of an objective quest meant to get to the heart of the story (Jennifer Smith Richards, personal interview, 2018).

When I interviewed Fox News commentator Juan Williams just weeks after NPR fired him for making what some viewed as anti-Muslim comments, my first question for him was, "You wrote for the *Washington*

Figure 5.2 Jennifer Smith Richards never apologizes for asking tough questions, knowing they were needed to get to the heart of a story.

Source: Jennifer Smith Richards

Figure 5.3 Interviewing is like a game of chess—don't ask a question until you have considered what answer may come from it, and what you might say next.

Source: Creative Commons/rawpixel.com

Post and have covered some of the biggest stories of our time, but you are now almost best known now for being fired by NPR. How do you feel about that?"

I knew he had talked about this topic ad nauseam, and I knew he was probably pretty annoyed that this single moment had (a) cost him his job and (b) was beginning to define what was actually a much broader and more accomplished career.

I wanted him to have the chance to have his say. His response: He laughed and later said he appreciated the fact I cut to the chase.

Sometimes, however, shaking things up can make sources uncomfortable.

I was writing a short piece on a new community education group advocating for enrollment in their local public schools (in a struggling district), as opposed to private, charter or suburban schools. Their view was the test scores for their district may be low, but these local schools measured up against any other institution in terms of the education and experience they provided.

I thought this would be a feel-good, 30-minute interview, but when I arrived I found myself seated at the head of a semi-circle, surrounded by nine organizers, all selling me their side of the issue. It made it almost impossible to get the focus and quotes I need.

Finally, I went on the offense, and challenged them with the poor reputation of their school district and the fact that a decent percentage of the students didn't graduate. Based on those facts, how would they sell me as a parent on staying in the district, based on the "success" of their neighborhood schools.

That resulted in some tremendous, impassioned comments about how they had built up their neighborhood schools—the exact quotes I needed to show the value of their organization.

I know I made them angry, but I also shook them from their script, and that was what my article needed (Kraft, 2014).

Chess Anyone?

I think of every interview like I am playing a game of chess. The key to chess is not just moving pieces—it is understanding how your opponent will react to your move and how you will react to their reaction. The same is true in interviewing.

In chess, if you make a move without thinking how your opponent will react to it, you will surely fail. Similarly, in interviewing, if you don't think ahead to what the answer will be to your question, you may, at best, simply not get the answer you want or need. At worst, you may be faced with an uncomfortable situation that alienates your subject.

Follow-Up Questions

Journalists new to interviewing ask a question furiously copy down the answer and then move on to the next question—regardless of the answer provide and whether their question has been answered or not.

Consider this example:

> *Reporter:* "Hi. I am writing a story on the charity bike ride for cancer. I am wondering who you are riding for."
>
> *Source:* "I'm riding for my aunt. She's been battling cancer on and off for about 10 years. She actually just got scans back this week and it's looking worse. I'm pretty worried about her."
>
> *Reporter:* "OK great! What's your training schedule like?"

A key part of asking questions is listening for the answers, and then escaping the confines of your script to probe further before moving on to another of your planned topics. It can also involve asking your question in another more probative way in the event it was not answered the first time. Following up can also involve a sympathetic response or acknowledgment of information previously provided.

Good follow-up questions require paying attention to what the source says in response to an initial question, and then allowing sources to converse further on subjects they have broached, even though you may not or may not have been planning to go there. Remember that you need to understand the issue or topic before you can ever share it with a reader, so some useful follow-up questions will include:

- "Would you tell me a bit more about that?"
- "Can you give me an example?"
- "How did you feel about that?"
- "Can you break that down a bit further in layman terms?"

A reporter's best technique can be to act far less informed than he or she may actually be. The second you let a source know that you have expertise, they can be inclined to jump ahead, skipping over key details (and quotes) that your story and reader will need.

Getting Off the Script

Everyone, even you, has a script. Think about a newsworthy story you tell about yourself that has been told repeatedly—how you broke your leg, picked your college, getting a big career opportunity. You have memorized the best way to tell that story and the truth as you recall it. But there is more to the story—how you felt, what you were thinking.

The first questions asked will usually result in recitation of the script. But if you keep asking more questions that allow the source to dig deeper into their own story, they will eventually leave the script and start providing more complex answers.

When a source answer from the script, notice how his or her is a bit sing-song. There will be noticeable peaks when the source hits on a point them have often made, and the story will have a recognizable rhythm. When they break free from that script, the voice will level out and often drops and octave or two.

Ask Original Question Again, Slightly Differently

More experienced sources know to answer the questions they wish they had been asked, as opposed to questions they are actually asked. That does not mean you need to abandon your questions and move on. Richard Davis, in a *Harvard Business Review* article, says to instead ask the same question twice, switching word orders or even acknowledging, "I know we talked about this a bit but I still need to know ..." (Davis, 2014).

There is no need to be confrontational, like "Look, I asked you this once but you didn't answer ..." Instead, give them the benefit of the doubt that they got sidetracked or misunderstood you. But you are also being clear you are not letting a source leave the subject without providing the answer readers need.

Box 5.4 Getting Past the Script

Mike Gulotta built his dream equine farm less than a decade after losing some of his closest friends and coworkers in the Sept. 11 terrorist attack. He had his script about where he was when the planes hit the tower and the aftermath, and his words were compelling. But I need him to dig a but deeper.

We had interviewed for several hours and he had told various aspects of his story, but I waited until he was outside his beautiful farm with friends and family, when I touched him on the arm and asked him: "Mike, looking at how far you have come since September 11, looking at these people who are here to share this moment with you, what does it feel like to be you?"

Here is what I wrote:

> It's a blue sky, 70-degree day at Deo Volente, and Mike Gulotta looks like a man who has everything. Wrapped in his arms is his grandson, Luke Michael, while Madeline, their two children and granddaughter mill about nearby. His friends and partners are there, admiring the facilities' amenities, petting the pretty horses, swaying to the music that cascades from overhead.
>
> It is a long way from the Manhattan of Sept. 11, 2001, but with one comment, a lone question, Gulotta returns to that moment of life-changing devastation and loss and salvation, and he is overcome with emotion so strong he can no longer speak.
>
> It takes just minutes for him to compose himself, but in that time it is clear that the man who put his faith in racing, his faith in this farm, his faith in his faith, has not been the same since that fateful day.
>
> "When you go through an event like that, you truly realize how precious life is, and the kind of impact that you have on people," Gulotta admitted, wiping his eyes. "It's a blessing to be here. And you try to do the best that you can do for other people—as long as you're alive. At this stage in my life, it's time to give of myself to help other people develop and grow and enrich their lives and realize their visions.
>
> "In order to inspire people to do that, you have to create the best."
>
> (Kraft, 2009)

Figure 5.4 Compassionate interviewing turned a story on a horse farm turned into a reflection on losses in the 9/11 terror attacks.

Source: *Hoof Beats*

Connect Answers with Active Listening

Active listening is a term that reflects the receiver of a message shows he or she is listening through body language or appropriate response. It is proof to someone talking that you have actually heard what they are saying and processed it. This is effective for all communication, but especially for interviewing. paraphrase what a source says to allow them to elaborate. "I hear you saying that business was tough during the recession. Walk me through what that meant for it to be tough."

Dig for the Implications

When your source says that his new company is providing better/different service than others in the same field, ask them how and why questions to better flush out the answer. Words are phrases are interpreted by those who hear/read them, and vague statements are open to broad interpretation. Statements like "It was nice to work for a company that cared," is really broad. What is nice? What does it mean to care. Unpack these answers so we all have the same idea and imagery.

Box 5.5 How Do You Ask That?

The Columbus Way

Kim Jacobs is the city's first gay, female police chief. But the new attitude she's bringing to the department has nothing to do with gender.

NICOLE KRAFT

PHOTOS BY JODI MILLER

Kimberley Jacobs was seeking a quick dinner when she stopped into the Ashland, Ohio, Pizza Hut.

What she found was a place in Columbus history.

In the summer of 1977, Jacobs, an Ohio State University sophomore majoring in natural resources, was eating with her family when she looked up to find a tall stranger standing military-straight by their table, looking at her and posing an even stranger question.

"Have you ever thought of a career in law enforcement?" he asked.

A 5-foot-8 hurdler on the Ohio State track team, Jacobs was young, lithe and athletic—which made the visitor, who turned out to be a lieutenant from the nearby Ohio State Patrol post, hope she might wish to be part of his unit's recruiting class. It was the heady days just after passage of Title IX and a bourgeoning women's rights movement was under way that, in Ashland at least, was focused on getting more females in police work.

Two months later, Jacobs was back at Ohio State, now as a sociology major, and her criminology courses soon sold her on the career that would take her to heights never before seen in Ohio—and barely seen anywhere in the country.

Figure 5.5 Columbus Police Chief Kim Jacobs's candor in a profile helped citizens better understand her life and career.
Source: *Columbus Monthly*

In a *Columbus Monthly* profile of Kimberley Jacobs, the fact she was named the chief of the Columbus, Ohio, police department—the first woman to hold that post—was the big angle that certainly made her newsworthy. But research showed a single reference in one story to the fact she had a partner named "Bobbi." As a female chief she was profile-worthy; as a lesbian chief of police, she was truly on the cutting edge, as there was only one other *ever* in the United States.

I could not, however, confirm her sexual orientation after numerous secondary interviews and hours of research. That led only one option: I had to ask her.

I struggled for days how to phrase the question and when to ask it in the course of my interview. It had to be toward the end, as I didn't want it to shape the whole session, but I had to have enough time to follow up on some questions within that framework. I also felt that blurting out, "Are you gay/a lesbian?" would make me sound at best insensitive and, at worst, like an idiot.

The chief actually gave me an opening in our first few minutes together when she told me she was working seven days a week, and how that was taking some getting used to. We were 45 minutes into our session and through much of her career—including her marriage to and divorce from a male fellow officer—before I followed up, asking her about her home life, and how her seven-day-a-week schedule impacted her family. She then mentioned her partner, Bobbi, and I did an internal happy dance when the chief used the pronoun "she."

Even then, I sought sensitivity, and my follow up was, "It sounds like your relationship with Bobbi makes you another first as a police chief in this city," to which she replied with a hearty laugh, "As far as we know."

We then had an extremely insightful conversation about what it means to be a lesbian in her role and what impact it might have on other women seeking equality in the future.

One way of asking a question could have made her defensive. The other way got amazing insights.

Source: Kraft (2012)

References

Curtis, C. (2018). LeBron James to Reporter: "You Should Be Like a Psychiatrist". June 7. Retrieved June 20, 2018, from https://ftw.usatoday.com/2018/06/nba-finals-cleveland-cavaliers-lebron-james-press-conference-reporter-psychiatrist-video.

Davis, R. (2014). Tactics for Asking Good Follow-Up Questions. November 14. Retrieved June 20, 2018, from https://hbr.org/2014/11/tactics-for-asking-good-follow-up-questions.

Kraft, N. (2009). God Willing: Faith, family and friendship bring Deo Volente Farms to life. *Hoof Beats*, April, 55–111.

Kraft, N. (2012). The Columbus Way: Kim Jacobs is the City's First Gay, Female Police Chief. But the New Attitude She's Bringing to the Department has Nothing to Do with Gender. *Columbus Monthly*, July.

Kraft, N. (2014). Clintonville Schools: Trying to Build a Community. *Columbus Monthly*, December.

Withers, T. (2005). LeBron James Ahead of His Time as a Player and as a Person. December 12. Retrieved June 20, 2018, from https://web.kitsapsun.com/archive/2005/12-12/83526_lebron_james_ahead_of_his_time_a.html.

Y-Press. (2009). Anatomy of a Question: John Sawatsky Part 1. November 20. Retrieved June 20, 2018, from https://vimeo.com/7726310.

6   Tricks of the Talking Trade

Charles Leerhsen recalls covering a Winter Olympics for Newsweek and speaking to teenage female ice skaters. While most reporters asked about their training and hopes for the competition, Leerhsen asked what they had brought with them to decorate their room at the Olympic Village.

"I couldn't get into their rooms, but I would ask every one of them, 'What do you have on your nightstand? What did you bring from home?' and then I would drop that into the story," he says. "My fellow reporters would think I snuck up into their room to see it, but I just had asked them for intimate and telling details" (personal interview, 2014).

While interviewing is often straightforward, it is also filled with tips and tricks that can help you get even more information from sources and move interviews forward even when they seem to have stalled.

Ask Around the Question

Even though you know the questions you need answered, don't be afraid to throw in some conversation starters that might take you in a more colorful direction. Leerhsen cited the example of asking a subject about their children which can, in turn, let them share something about their home life:

> Even if they have one child, say, "Well your house in the morning must be but must be crazy." If you're talking to Jay-Z and Beyonce, they might say, "Well, it's not so bad. You know we actually have four maids …"
>
> You get an insight into their house, if you sound sympathetic. It's an innocent question. You're not prying, but you just might get the person talking about their home or a typical morning.
>
> (Charles Leerhsen, personal interview, 2014)

Figure 6.1 Charles Leerhsen has interviewed celebrities, public officials and sports figures for publications like *People, US Weekly* and *Sports Illustrated*, and says one of his best interviewing tools is simple silence.

Source: Charles Leerhsen

It's OK to Appear Stupid

There are moments when pretending you know less than you do may encourage sources to open up and provide more information.

Mac McClelland does not "pretend on purpose" to be stupid, but people have come to that conclusion because McClelland did not look old enough to be a reporter and often spoke in a casual vernacular that caught people off guard:

> I use interjections, and I occasionally "up" talk. I have a very casual way of speaking, in general and … people are like "mmm this person is probably not that bright." As a result, source will provide more unguarded information, since they do not feel they are talking to a wily journalist.
>
> (Mac McClelland, personal interview, 2014)

Rinse and Repeat

There are interview subjects who have a clear agenda in mind, or are blinded by their own message, and will ignore your question (maybe intentionally, maybe not), and provide an answer they feel compelled to give.

Consider a favorite campus pizza spot, closing because the building owner decided to renovate the space and rent it to a chain that could pay higher rents. Questions to the landlord about how and why the change is taking place, and the impact on campus, might get a party line about enhancing the neighborhood, but don't give up. You can re-ask the question with active listening: "I hear and respect what you are saying about gentrifying the area, but I really need to know what the impact may be on campus to have this business leave the area."

You can also rephrase the question with your active listening: "There has been a lot of new development in the campus area. Let's talk about what impact the changes in this area will mean for students, the university and the community."

Wrangling

Many interview subjects like to talk—a lot. And sometimes what they want to talk about goes way off topic from your story's subject. You don't want to offend a rambling subject by cutting them off, but you also need to get your story back on track.

Try letting them go for a minute or two, and then try to get them refocused:

- "That is so interesting. Could we just backtrack a bit. . . ."
- "I completely hear what you are saying, but just to come back to this topic . . ."

Rebooting

Sometimes interviews go off track and, try as you might, your subject refuses to join you on the topic. Or you may realize after an interview starts that this source just is not right for this article. It that case, don't be afraid to cut bait. By all means, thank your subject for their help and chat a little—but keep your recorder still running.

After some small talk, suggest you forgot to ask a question and try to get the interview restarted.

Silence Is Golden

Human beings abhor a lull in conversation. We feel uncomfortable and are compelled to fill it with words. That makes this a glorious journalistic tool. If you have asked a question and your source answered superficially, just keep looking at them expectantly and don't ask another question.

Inexperienced subjects will get nervous and keep talking, often providing the best quote. Even people who have been interviewed many times and have answers that are practiced and canned can be enticed to go "off script" if you just wait for five seconds after they finish their last sentence without saying anything.

That moment of silence will get them thinking and they'll start speaking more thoughtfully and with another perspective.

Charles Leerhsen has interviewed celebrities, public officials and sports figures for publications like *People, US Weekly* and *Sports Illustrated*, and says one of his best interviewing tools is simple silence:

> Silence is an important tool in an interview, especially when you get to difficult questions. With so many subjects these days there is a scandal in their past or an embarrassing moment or a failure that has to be broached in the course of the reporting. When you get to that point, sometimes they have a prepared answer or they just slough it off. Very often you can just let them say that and then just try saying nothing, letting a few beats go by, and seeing if they don't jump in at that very important moment and add something.
>
> (Charles Leerhsen, personal interview, 2014)

Another technique he uses was borrowed from Mike Wallace of *60 Minutes* fame:

> He said if he heard something that sounded like a prepared answer or BS, he'd say "Really?" That was his follow. He had a lot of heat with that little pivot, and he got a lot of very important people—kings and princes— stuttering and fumbling and trying to assure him that that it was true. In the process they revealed something about their honesty if nothing else.
>
> (Charles Leerhsen, personal interview, 2014)

Wallace is also most famous for showing interviewing the ambush interview— confronting subjects suddenly, and without warning, a targeted interview subject. The goal was to get spur-of-the-moment responses on controversial topics.

Ambush journalism became a controversial tactic that many journalists deemed unethical. Wallace later abandoned the style after they provided more drama than quality content. It lives on, however, in some celebrity journalism.

No Comment

Try as you might to get an answer, the fact is some sources (politicians, coaches, polished sources) simply won't answer your question or address the issue you've raised or may not even return your calls. The only option we have then is to let the reader know we tried.

If you asked a question and it was not answered, or a source declined to comment, write "John Doe declined to comment when asked ..."

If you try to reach a source on a tight deadline and they don't get back to you, you can say they were "not available for comment."

If you try to reach a source repeatedly and you know they are ducking your calls, tell the reader, "John Doe did not respond to repeated attempts for comment."

Burning bridges is a concern, but the truth is the truth. The readers need to know you did your best on their behalf to get the information, and your source was not willing to accommodate.

Be Interested

Give people a chance to talk about what interests them. If you know a mortgage broker has a classic car museum, ask him about it, even though it doesn't fit your story on how interest rates are impacting mortgages.

Sports writer Jeff Pearlman, who wrote for *Sports Illustrated*, says tattoos can be a point of contact with a source:

> They tell so many stories. Every time I see a guy with a tattoo, I'm like, "What's that tattoo for?" And he may respond, "My daughter died when she was an infant." Really!? All of the sudden you're not just writing about the wide receiver for Ohio State, you're writing about a wide receiver for Ohio State who lost his daughter and wears it on his arm.
>
> (Jeff Pearlman, personal interview, 2017)

Box 6.1 Five Steps to an Intimate Interview

Lane DeGregory offers these steps for maximizing interview time.

- **Check them out**

  - Who is this person? Do they have a criminal record, guns, voting, boats, cars, blogs, Facebook, YouTube?
  - Why do you want to talk to them: Why are you doing this story? Who cares? Why does this person matter?
  - What do you hope to get out of them? Other leads? Connections? Insight?
  - What do you need to know: Family, personality, pets, interests, accomplishments, discomforts, downfalls.

- **Make your move**

  - Establish credibility, character, why they should trust you.
  - Plan your pitch: Call, do not email, talk on their turf —"When can I come over?"

- Get your toe in the door.
- Talk about talking: Explain intentions. What's in it for them? What do they have to lose? What are they worried about? Show stories, bring a friend, no photographer, no interference, no notes.

• Put them at ease

  - Make connections: Dress the part, watch shoes, jewelry, vehicle.
  - Be honest about understanding: insider, expert, idiot.
  - Find common ground, aim for conversation: dogs, kids, cars.
  - Be attentive: Small talk, big ears, eye contact, body language, encouragement.
  - Savor silence, shut up and nod, let them fill the void.
  - Be fascinated, interested, concerned, confused, accepting—don't judge!
  - Observe as well as interview: Ironed v. disheveled, make-up and manicure, tattoos. See, smell, listen, taste, feel, think, wonder.
  - Body language, expressions, things unanswered or unsaid.
  - Fly on the wall: When they wake, eat, work, play, parent, chill before bed.

• Get intimate

  - Emotional appeal, empathy, compassion, shared experience, understanding.
  - Pieces of the past: Tour the house, framed photos, souvenirs, trophies, scrapbooks, albums.
  - Written words: Journals? Diaries? Love letters? Cards? Emails? To-do lists? Meaning in details.
  - Share yourself: The first time I was lonely, lost someone, took off my wedding ring. I can't imagine what you're going through; help me understand.
  - What do you want to ask me? What do you want to make sure I know?
  - A mile in their moccasins: Put yourself in their shoes emotionally, situationally, what would you do?
  - Sit beside them or below them: don't fear the floor or the bait bucket.

- **Morning after**

  - Get their cell, leave your sweater.
  - Call me any time, if you think of anything.
  - When can I see you again? Church? Dinner? Drive?
  - Other ways to contact you, meet your friends, parents.
  - I'll bring that book by.
  - Always forget something . . .

Figure 6.2 Pulitzer winner Lane DeGregory believes reporting with heart is a key part of her success.

Source: Lane DeGregory

Source: Lane DeGregory, email interview, 2018

Holly Zachariah of the *Columbus Dispatch* recalls reporting on the City of Marysville plan to build a new $20 million sewer plant. She knew the plant itself was "not an interesting story even on my worst day," but there had to be a way to bring the story to life. She started thinking about the neighbors not liking the smell, and how the plant might combat that. She soon discovered the guy whose job it is to spend every minute of his day over the anaerobic digesters:

> He has to make sure it's doing its job and not stinking more than it should. If you go in thinking, "Why does this guy want to work in a sewer plant and what is so interesting about it?," and knowing that for

Figure 6.3 Holly Zachariah says finding a person to bring a story to life can make even the most mundane topics interesting.

Source: Jonathan Quilter/*Columbus Dispatch*

hours he can tell you everything you've ever wanted to know about a sewer plant, and it is the most exciting four hours that man has had in weeks, because nobody ever wants to hear him talk about sewage. That's not being a jerk; that's you recognizing people are giving you their story and the time of day, and you find some connection with them.

(Holly Zachariah, personal interview, 2018)

Another useful trick is to give people a chance at the end to put into the story what they wish by asking, "Is there anything else we need to know about this?"

I profiled someone who had spent his entire career in human resources at Ohio State and was now receiving a Lifetime Achievement Award days before his retirement. After an hour discussing his life and career, I asked him at the end of our interview, "Is there anything else you think we should know?"

His response: "Well, it's funny, but I was actually born at Ohio State Hospital, in the same wing where my office is now. I guess it's time I finally left the nest."

That became both my lead and the article's closing quote, and I never would have thought to ask that question.

Reveal a Bit of Yourself

If it will make your subject feel more comfortable, don't be afraid to reveal a bit about yourself in the interview.

Charles Leerhsen says:

> Maybe someone lost a loved one or something personal or painful, and if you think in the moment it would help them feel more comfortable to get a sense of you understanding maybe a little bit what they're going through to show some empathy then I think it makes sense to share just a little bit of yourself. If you happen to mention, "I have some idea how you feel—my father died, too," they may feel like "OK, I can talk about this. I actually feel safe."
>
> (Charles Leerhsen, personal interview, 2014)

Pulitzer Prize winner Lane DeGregory recalls covering commercial fishing when she was noticeably pregnant. The conversation became as much about her belly as it did fishing. She says that changed her from being a reporter hiding behind a notepad to being a human being connecting with people.

"I had to become comfortable with talking about myself a bit more," she admits. "It was a big turning point for me. If people see me as mom and dog owner, it rounds me out a bit more" (personal interview, 2018).

Box 6.2 Walking through Time and Memory

Gathering quotes for a straightforward news story is a skill that comes fairly quickly with some practice. What is more challenging is getting facts and quotes related to longer form pieces: extensive profiles, exposes, investigative pieces, recreations.

For those stories we need to really plot out the course of the interview and how to walk sources through given subjects or moments in time.

In these interviews, we start slowly and use the bell-curve model to work toward a crescendo, with our most difficult questions coming at the peak of the curve, or even slightly past the peak.

Consider a story about a young, successful businessman named Brian Pinske who died at age 36 in a hotel room during a business trip, due to an accidental overdose of pain medication and alcohol. His parents, who were on the same trip, and had dinner with him the night before, discovered his body.

Four years later, I was writing a look back at how his business had carried on after his death and felt the story needed to recreate the shocking circumstances of his passing to be able to explore his life. That meant asking his mother, Marlys, to relive the last time she saw him and her discovery of his body. I had never met her before, and she asked we talk at a hotel. We spent a total of five hours on the interview, and here is how it broke down:

Part 1: We got to know each other and I let her ramble—how their family business was going now, stories about her grandchild. I also asked her to tell me about her son. What he was like, stories about him growing up—good memories and good background that I may or may not use for the piece.

Part 2: I started to ask her about the night he died. She told me how they had been sitting together in the hotel bar, and she said goodnight to him before she went up to bed. The next morning she found him dead. It's all great information, but there are huge holes that I needed to walk her through so she could fill in. I started by asking her to take me back to the bar, and then we talked about.

- Who else was with you?
- Where were you standing when you said goodnight?
- Show me how you rubbed your hand on his back.
- Describe for me the last time you looked down into his face—what do you remember?
- What did he say?
- What did you say?
- What time did you go to bed?

I didn't pepper her like an interrogation. I leaned forward, tilted my head, and tried to help her see the scene in her mind. Each question took her further back in time, and it was like a paint-by-numbers. I gave her the number in question form, and she filled in the details piece by piece until I could see the whole picture. If I needed more detail, I asked her to describe a moment in time—even something as personal as, "Walk me through the morning you found him, as you approached his hotel room. What did the door sound like when you used the key? What was it like when you walked into the room. Show me."

Part 3: We were like old friends, and she shared with me private family moments, deep memories, details.
Here is how part of the lede turned out:

> Marlys had bid Brian goodnight from the Marriott Hotel bar at 12:30 a.m., rubbing her hand up and down his broad back as she stood by where he sat. He looked up at her with gentle blue eyes, his sandy brown hair softly spiked away from his forehead.

"I'll see you in the morning, Mom," he said with a smile.

Less than 12 hours later, she stood outside her son's hotel room —the one adjoining her own—keycard in hand.

Tim thought Brian might have gotten up early and gone out, but Marlys heard the television playing through the door. They had wanted to call, yet did not wish to awaken him should sleep be what he needed.

She had waited long enough.

She inserted the key into the door slot and felt the click of the lock releasing.

She eased down the handle and stepped into the dimness of the room. Brian lay on his back on the bed. There was no rhythm of breath, no glow to his cheeks—only the tinny sound of the television in the too-still room.

Marlys Pinske began to scream.

(Kraft, 2006)

If you don't get there on the first try, no problem. Just kept circling us back, digging out detail, asking for more elaboration, with more specific and focused questions.

Figure 6.4 Brian Pinske's mother, Marlys, spent several hours sharing the story of her son's last day after we had built a relationship during our interview.

Source: *Hoof Beats*

Let Your Subject Drive

Reporters most often start an interview with their own well-constructed questions. What about letting the subject drive the interview, suggests Lane DeGregory, by asking, "What would you like to talk about?"

"Let the person drive the bus a little while," she says. "Letting them feel like they are in control gives them confidence that starting with your own questions doesn't."

DeGregory also advocates letting subjects bring someone along to the interview if they wish.

"That way you may get dialogue instead of quotes," she says. "They can challenge, interact, tease, even call 'bullshit.' It really does help" (personal interview, 2018).

Create a Reason to Return

DeGregory says she has made a habit of buying dollar-store reading glasses —and it's not just to read her notes. Instead she leaves a pair behind as a guarantee she will be able to get back in the door of even the most challenging source.

"I never know if I have pissed them off they that they won't let me back in," she says. "If leave my glasses, they will never tell me I can't come back. It's a nice in if I need to do that" (personal interview, 2018).

Be Relentless

Sources will give you superficial answers, or they may not give you an answer at all. *Do not give up!* Be polite, but firm. Acknowledge they don't want to talk but say you have a job to do, and that job is to get this information. You want to be fair. You want to be accurate. All you ask is they work with you.

"Sometimes you have to be antagonistic," DeGregory says. "You don't want people to use empathy to your disadvantage" (personal interview, 2018).

Have Heart

Reporters are often taught to be impartial and pursue just the facts, but Holly Zachariah says the key to her reporting success is that she never forgets the people she interviews are humans with real human emotions:

> I'm always the reporter who gets teased a lot, because I'm the one who's crying. I'm the one standing in the back of the courtroom in tears. I'm the one pulling out my tissues at the interview, and there's

no shame in that game. I think it's what helps make me better at what I do.

You also have to never lose sight of the reporter relationship. "I'm here to tell your story, and we need to remember that," so it is a balance. It weighs heavy on my mind and the mind of any good journalist. A lot of your stories are very tragic stories. They're full of emotion. As the reporter that cries in a courtroom, [I] think you're almost capturing your own emotion through writing that story. I check myself every day.

(Holly Zachariah, personal interview, 2018)

Box 6.3 "Your Job There Is to Listen"

Jeff Pearlman was a 27-year-old writer at *Sports Illustrated* in 1999 when he was sent to profile John Rocker during the Braves-Mets National League Championship Series. Rocker, a pitcher for the Braves, was considered "outlandish" and a bit of a "lunkhead."

Pearlman had limited access but managed some interviews with the subject and his parents, and planned to write about Rocker, the misunderstood guy. He recalls:

> With Rocker, I made a huge mistake. I went in, and in stories he seemed like a dick, but he's really a nice guy. That's the story I wrote, and I submitted the story to Sports Illustrated—John Rocker misunderstood. The closing passage of that story was John Rocker, 10 years old, his dog dying in his arms, and John Rocker crying. That was the last image of him in the story. It was this real puff-piece thing.
>
> (Jeff Pearlman, personal interview, 2017)

But the New York Yankees ended up sweeping the Braves in the World Series, so *Sport Illustrated* held the story. Instead, Pearlman's editor suggested during the off season that Pearlman go down to Georgia to freshen up the Rocker story, and see if he could spend more time with him.

Pearlman flew down to Atlanta and was picked up by Rocker. The rest is journalistic history, as Pearlman succeeded in writing an explosive profile that some say led to the end of Rocker's career:

> He picks me up on the side of the road and we're driving down the highway, and in front of us there's a car that's moving slowly. Rocker goes, "Fucking Asian women, they fucking cannot drive. God fucking damn it." We drive past the car and it's a white woman driving the car, which was delicious.

Then we get up to the tollbooth and it's one of those tollbooths you have to throw money in. He throws change in. He throws some more change in, it doesn't open it. Someone behind us starts honking. Rocker rolls down the window, sticks out the middle finger, "Fuck you." Then he spits on the tollbooth. He literally hocks back a loogie and spits on the tollbooth. Finally, it gets opened.

We're driving, I'm hanging out with him on the day he's speaking to a school for disadvantaged children. His agent set it up. I'm like, "Do you enjoy doing this?" He's like, "Fuck no. I hate this shit, but my agent wants me to do it."

(Jeff Pearlman, personal interview, 2017)

Throughout the day, Rocker revealed himself in the most extraordinary of ways, Pearlman recalls:

He hates everyone. He's awful. There is a lesson here. Seriously, you cannot pick a worse guy to have in the car [with you] if you're John Rocker. Not only am I an up-and-coming reporter who believes in reporting and interviewing, not only do I have a tape recorder and pen with me, but I'm this liberal Jew who's going to show you no sympathy whatsoever even if you wanted it. You picked the wrong guy here.

The key is I never argued with him, I never debated with him, I never egged him on. Your job there is to listen. Your entire job is to get information and to find out who this person is. He's literally revealing himself in front of you; he's showing you who he is. That's gold.

(Jeff Pearlman, personal interview, 2017)

Here is Pearlman's lede:

A minivan is rolling slowly down Atlanta's Route 400, and John Rocker, driving directly behind it in his blue Chevy Tahoe, is pissed. "Stupid bitch! Learn to f—-ing drive!" he yells. Rocker honks his horn. Once. Twice. He swerves a lane to the left.

There is a toll booth with a tariff of 50 cents. Rocker tosses in two quarters. The gate doesn't rise. He tosses in another quarter. The gate still doesn't rise. From behind, a horn blasts. "F—-you!" Rocker yells, flashing his left middle finger out the window. Finally, after Rocker has thrown in two dimes and a nickel, the gate rises. Rocker brings up a thick wad of phlegm. Puuuh! He spits at the machine. "Hate this damn toll."

With one hand on the wheel, the other gripping a cell phone, Rocker tears down the highway, weaving through traffic. In 10 minutes he is due to speak at Lockhart Academy, a school for learning-disabled children. Does Rocker enjoy speaking to children? "No," he says, "not really." But of all things big and small he hates—New York Mets fans, sore arms, jock itch—the thing he hates most is traffic. "I have no patience," he says.

The speedometer reads 72. Rocker, in blue-tinted sunglasses and a backward baseball cap, is seething. "So many dumb asses don't know how to drive in this town," he says, Billy Joel's "New York State of Mind" humming softly from the radio. "They turn from the wrong lane. They go 20 miles per hour. It makes me want—Look! Look at this idiot! I guarantee you she's a Japanese woman." A beige Toyota is jerking from lane to lane. The woman at the wheel is white. "How bad are Asian women at driving?"

(Pearlman, 1999)

Figure 6.5 Jeff Pearlman said the key to his legendary interview with pitcher John Rocker was, "I never argued with him, I never debated with him, I never egged him on."

Source: Jeff Pearlman

References

Kraft, N. (2006). The Life of Brian: Brian Pinske Has Been Gone almost Four Years, but His Influence and Memory Live On. *Hoof Beats*, October, 72–86.

Pearlman, J. (1999) At Full Blast: Shooting Outrageously from the Lip, Braves Closer John Rocker Bangs Away at his Favorite Targets: The Mets, Their Fans, Their City and Just about Everyone in It. *Sports Illustrated*, December 27.

7 Covering Sports

In the classic baseball film *Bull Durham*, catcher Crash Davis sits on the team bus with rising star pitcher Nuke LaLoosh, and tells him, "It's time to work on your interview. Learn your clichés. You have to study them, you have to have to know them. They are your friends."

His instruction begins:

"We've got to play them one game at a time."

LaLoosh repeats and then comments, "It's kind of boring."

"Of course, it's boring," Davis replies. "That's the point. Write it down."

Davis offers more quotes:

"I'm just happy to be here. I hope I can help the ball club.

"I just want to give it my best shot and, the Good Lord willing, things will work out."

(Shelton, 1988)

Sports are the ultimate reality show, with high stakes, buildup of tensions and excitement, and definitive winners and losers. They can also be filled with clichéd moments like the scene from *Bull Durham*.

But the high emotions that make sports such powerful storytelling, combined with the restrictive nature of the sports industry, can make interviews some of the best, and some of the most challenging.

"When you're playing well it's great to have cameras in front of your face, it's real easy to be excited about what you do," says former Major League pitcher Dan Plesac, now a broadcaster with the MLB Network. "But when you stink or have that game that's the bad side of it, when you have to talk about what went wrong, that's a much tougher interview" (personal interview, 2017).

Sports interviews are often heavily managed affairs that take place in their own specialized environments, including:

- **Press conferences:** A favorite information dissemination tool for teams from college to the pros. There is often a regularly scheduled session with coaches and players at set times after practice, and the leagues set

Figure 7.1 Interviewing athletes can be exciting and extraordinarily challenging, due to the constraints placed on reporters by teams.

Source: Nicole Kraft

requirements for post-game press access. This allows large quantities of reporters to ask questions of a single person (or a few people) at one point in time. Questions are asked (and answers received) in a group setting, with reporters in an audience and sources at a podium or behind a table. Media relations personnel determine who asks questions (and in what order), and stop the session after a given period of time.

- **Scrum:** A rugby term describing a formation of players that starts play. In sports, it is the crowd of journalists that gather around a player during media availability or post-game locker-room comments. It's almost like a mini, less formal press conference, in that as each person's question and the subsequent answer is open to the crowd, but you are closer to a subject and often media relations personnel are not managing the interaction.
- **One-On-One:** Individual interviews with players or coaches, often scheduled through media relations departments or sports information directors. They will coordinate the time and length of the interview and may even sit in, depending on the team, player and circumstance.

Tom Withers, a sports writer with the Associated Press in Cleveland, admits the management of locker rooms has become "insufferable," and

Figure 7.2 The scrum, unique to sports, gathers numerous reporters around a single subject for "media availability."

Source: Nicole Kraft

says media relations have instead become "player protection." It takes building relationships to get around those controls:

> It takes patience and understanding of subject. What you have seen reflected in March Madness is how emotions have such become a huge part of the interview process. That's why there is a 10-minute cooling off period after a game. People let their hearts get attached to games—fans, players and journalists.
>
> (Tom Withers, personal interview, 2018)

Successful sports interviewing means working within the given parameters and maximizing the opportunities provided. Before you head out to the stadium or field, it's important to understand some key aspects of sports reporting and the rules by which we cover teams.

Check Your Fandom at the Door

"Coach, I have this girlfriend who is a huge Iowa fan, and I would make major points with her if you could sign this" (Petchesk, 2013).

So begins one of the most uncomfortable videos ever viewed by journalism students, as Ed Littler, sports director at News 5 in Nebraska, asked Iowa coach Kirk Ferentz for an autograph during 2011 Big Ten media days. Littler is now legendary in sports media classes for this interchange, which overstepped the bounds of reporter and sports figure.

When you enter sports reporting, you are no longer a fan, and you can't act like one. Rule No. 1 of sports writing is, "There is no cheering in the press box," and rule No. 2 is there is no public displays of affection for those you cover—be they individuals or teams.

That does not mean you ask only professional and business-minded questions. Remember that this is a conversation, and athletes are people, too. You can ask how was their day, or congratulate them on a good game. But your goal remains to get information for readers in a fair and objective manner.

Do Your Homework

Do your research on whomever you're going to interview, because if you don't make that athlete or that coach feel comfortable, you're not going to get anything back.

"There's nothing worse than going and interviewing someone and you're not prepared because he senses it right away, and then you sense that he's uncomfortable, and then you have no chance of going anywhere with the interview," says Dan Plesac.

Figure 7.3 Dan Plesac says waiting on players and coaches for interviews can be frustrating, but it is part of the sports writing game.

Source: Dan Plesac

He cited the example of interviewing a starting forward on a men's college basketball team:

> Know the guy's name, know what high school he went to, know the position he plays, instead of going, "I notice your last game you scored 18 points, were you surprised?" And the guy is going to look at you and go, "Hell no! I scored 25 from the game before and 36 games before that."
>
> (Dan Plesac, personal interview, 2017)

Being prepared can be as simple as an internet search, says Alison Lukan of *The Athletic*. "Google their name, look at the headlines," she says. "These are proud athletes. They have worked their butts off to get to where they are, and I think it's a very easy way to start to build a rapport by acknowledging that you know something about them. Feed their ego" (personal interview, 2018).

Homework also helps reporters separate themselves from the pack, whether it is asking a truly unique question in a press conference or finding an original angle to a game story.

"No two games are ever the same," says Withers:

> When you go tonight you might see LeBron score 65 or Kevin Love get hurt again. The more you are prepared, the more likely you are to see the story when it unfolds and see what makes it stand a part. In the 24/7 news cycle, you have to look for that emotional component. Two days are never the same.
>
> (Tom Withers, personal interview, 2018)

Your Knowledge Is Not that Important

Every sports writer has heard someone at a press conference ask a question like: "So coach, why did you move out of the 2–3 defense midway through the first half?" To which the coach may reply, "What are you talking about?" Or there may be the question that takes 30 seconds to state, meandering through the reporter's vast array of knowledge. Before you ask such questions, stop yourself, says Withers:

> Take a step back and realize you are not an expert. You may have played basketball in high school. Maybe you have watched every NFL game over five years. What you know and think is not really important. Your question needs to get your sources to say what they know and think.
>
> (Tom Withers, personal interview, 2018)

Appearance

Most sports writers I know dress comfortably but professionally, straddling business casual. The obvious dress code for a sports interview is no jerseys or spirit wear—for or against the team you are visiting. When I cover a Columbus Blue Jackets NHL game I don't even wear blue. Yet during the NBA playoffs—and hours before the NFL draft—Joe Vardon of Cleveland. com wore a Tim Couch Cleveland Browns jersey to a Cavaliers media session. The response from LeBron James: "I can't take you seriously wearing that" (Davies, 2018).

Plesac was not surprised by the response, as he says players actually judge reporters by how they dress and how they present themselves to players:

> If you walk up to a player and your dress sloppy and you look sloppy, first of all that player or that coach, they are not going to take you seriously from the beginning. They're going to look at you as like some local guy that's here, that doesn't know what he's supposed to be doing and you're just asking some random questions.

Box 7.1 Vardon Explains His Jersey

After viewing the photo of Joe Vardon in his Browns jersey, Ohio State journalism student Zach Varda reached out to ask his motivation, and what were the rules around such a public display of fandom. He shared with this emailed response from Vardon:

> You cannot wear any gear of the team you are covering or a team in the league (conference, division, level) you are covering for a game or practice, or really anywhere outside of your home (pajamas are OK). I actually have bad dreams about that, going to like an Indians game to cover it or something and I'm wearing an Indians t-shirt.
>
> What I did with wearing a Browns-Tim Couch jersey to a Cavs morning workout was way, way, way different. People wear sports gear to practice all the time, so long as it is not of the team they cover. In my particular case, I was wearing the Couch jersey because it was the day before the NFL draft, and I was making satirical commentary on the Browns' bad drafting of quarterbacks, given that they were about to take one No. 1.
>
> Here's the truth: whatever you've been told about this—keep doing it. You're young and you're just starting out, you're looking for a way in and a way to be noticed. Don't let your clothes be the thing that gets you passed over for a job. If you're me, and you've

covered presidential elections for the *Columbus Dispatch*, and you've spent the last four years chronicling one of the most recognizable athletes in the world, and you've had this long career in a tough business, you can let your hair down a little when you're going to a morning practice toward the end of a nine-month season (I covered my 100th game this season on Tuesday).

By the time you reach the point where I am in your career, your readers and the subjects you cover will know you are fair and impartial by your writing and the questions you ask them. They'll fear you and respect you. And they'll laugh when you wear a silly Browns jersey (that night—for the game—I was dressed to the 9s, full suit, pocket square, tie bar, polished shoes).

Source: Joe Vardon, email response to Zach Varda, May 18, 2018 (reprinted with permission)

Figure 7.4 Press conferences allow reporters to have access to key sources like Ohio State coach Urban Meyer, but time and type of questions are limited.

Source: Nicole Kraft

Sports Is on Player Time

If you work in sports, you will likely alternate between chasing and waiting on coaches and players. I once drove for 2½ hours to Cleveland to interview a player visiting with the Los Angeles Dodgers, for a magazine article. I was told to arrive at 4 p.m. for a pre-game sit down —and sit I did. From 4 p.m. until 6. Then I was told his pre-game ritual had begun, and he was no longer available.

"Sometimes it's really hard to swallow that you have an appointment lined up with the women's soccer coach at Ohio State, and it's going to be at 7:30 in the morning and you get there at 7:30 and she doesn't get there till 9, you have to accept that you are on their schedule," Plesac says. "You're wanting their time, and they don't necessarily look at your time being as important as their time. That's the hardest thing to swallow, and you can't question it because you need them more than they need you" (personal interview, 2017).

Box 7.2 Reporting on Player Time

Dan Plesac says interviewing athletes can be both challenging and frustrating. He related this experience from one interview quest:

I was doing a report on a team, and I needed one last guy. The PR department told me he would be ready at 8:30 a.m. At 8:30 I'm ready, and I see him coming out, and he sees me and he tells me "I got to go do some early work. I'll be back in like half hour." OK. I know they are on the field at 10 a.m., and once the work out starts at 10, I'm not getting him, because he'll be on the field from 10 until the game at 1.

What happens is he slips by and gets on to the field, and now I'm not going to get him until about 12:45. I have about a 15-minute window, because we start taping the show at 1 p.m.

It's hard not to get angry and when I see him coming off the field, and I'm like, "I need to get you for two minutes," and they give you the role of the eyes. You feel taken back a little bit. You almost want to say, "Hey, I don't want to kiss your ass to do this." You can't say that. So then when he walks over, and he kind of he's like not into it at all. And there's nothing worse than interviewing somebody who is completely non-engaged.

I started with, "Tell me about your off season—you guys made a lot of changes," and I get this response: "Yeah we did." So I'm like, "You've have four terrific years in a row—what does a guy like you do in the off season to prepare? Any kind of different prep?"

"Nope same."

One word answer, right?

I say "Did you do anything different this reason? More weight lifting?" And his response was, "What are you saying, I'm not in shape?"

I know now it's going nowhere. You can't make something out of nothing. Every one of these soundbites suck, and they are not going to use any of it. So then I just said, "Well listen, a lot of people pick you guys to win the Central Division. How do you feel about it?"

That kind of perked him up and he was like, "You know every year we always think we're going to have a good team, and this year's the same way. We made some changes."

Finally. Something I can use.

Source: Dan Plesac, personal interview, 2017

Be Adaptable

Tom Withers was at a Cavaliers press conference before the 2017/18 season, not long after an emotionally charged trade that sent Kyrie Irving to the Boston Celtics. It also happened to be the same day LeBron James tweeted to President Donald Trump regarding the "revocation" of an invitation for NBA champion Golden State Warriors to visit the White House. James's tweet read: "U bum @StephenCurry30 already said he ain't going! So therefore ain't no invite. Going to White House was a great honor until you showed up!" (James, 2017).

Withers, the senior Cavs writer, is honored with the first question at the team's media gatherings, and he planned to ask about that tweet. But James cut him off.

"Tom," he said. "I know you want to talk about a lot of subjects. Stay on one before we move on."

Withers then invited James to talk about what he wanted to talk about. Withers recalls:

He talked about Kyrie. You can't get yourself locked into one thing. You have to be adaptable—change on the fly and respond to wherever the subject takes you. I had gone through seven or eight things I wanted to address, and I had them ready in my head wherever he wasn't going to take it.

(Tom Withers, personal interview, 2018)

Don't Kill the Rally

Sports interview challenges are not always the fault of the team or player. The rigidity of new or inexperienced reporters can blind them to the challenges in their question or interview style, such as the "rally-killer" question.

According to Tom Withers:

> Young journalists often ... have blinders on. They don't understand how the flow of the interview is going. We will get a subject going on a game or an injury, and then someone asks a question from left field. It stops the whole interview in its track. You have to be perceptive of what's happening around you and what's being discussed.
>
> (Tom Withers, personal interview, 2018)

Withers also mentioned the interviewer who goes on and on (and on) to prove their own knowledge, instead of letting their subject do the talking.

Dan Plesac admits that when he started broadcasting, he'd often find his questions rambling, to the detriment of his audience:

> The hardest thing for me to do when I got into broadcasting was ask a direct question. Like if I was interviewing [a coach], I'd take five minutes to go over the Indiana football game from last week. I would start to say, "Hey, you had kind of a little bit of a struggle, close game at the fourth quarter and I know it was a one-touchdown game going into the fourth quarter. Were you surprised?" You're trying to let [the coach] know that you know what you are talking about. But in reality, he knows that.
>
> Instead of going on with a long-winded question about the Indiana game, it's better to be short and say, "The Indiana game was a struggle. Why do you think that was the case?" And let him talk. Because the viewer at home and the person listening on the radio, they don't want to hear you.
>
> (Dan Plesac, personal interview, 2017)

Learning to Look and Listen

Listening may appear to be a lost art, especially in sports interviews, but Withers says it is among the most important skills for a reporter to develop:

> With all due respect to the broadcast folks, a lot of [broadcast] is monologues with questions. It's not about you. It's about not hearing yourself and instead hearing what people are saying. You may go into interview questions you may want to ask but be open to hearing what people are saying. And be open to new line of questioning, even a new story.
>
> (Tom Withers, personal interview, 2018)

Alison Lukan recalls a press conference where the press pool thought a hockey player was going to be scratched from the game, but the coach confirmed he would, in fact, be on the ice: "This person just kept continuing with their line of questioning like the player wouldn't be in the game," Lukan says. "I feel like there are people who aren't engaged in a whole discussion in a scrum or a press conference" (personal interview, 2018).

Tom Withers advocates capturing how questions are answered, in addition to the words expressed, to take the reader places he or she can't go:

> Talk about in the locker room when someone kicked the trash can. Or the tears streaming down cheeks of sophomore guard who missed the game-winning jumper. Or swallowing hard before answering a question. Or an eye roll. All these little things create a narrative to draw people in. We get to see how people feel in some of the most raw, emotional times they have as athletes. Try and convey that in the story.
>
> (Tom Withers, personal interview, 2018)

Figure 7.5 Columbus Blue Jackets head coach John Tortorella gives some post press conference time to Tom Reed of *The Athletic.*

Source: Nicole Kraft

Avoid the Pack

Whether it's sports, politics or covering a fire, look for ways to separate from the media masses and get your own materials.

Jeff Pearlman recalls being the No. 2 baseball writer at *Sports Illustrated* behind Tom Verducci, and he would always watch how the more legendary baseball writer worked the clubhouse:

> Let's say it was the Yankees back in the late' 90s. The clubhouse would open and all the reporters would flock to Derek Jeter. Verducci would hover around, and he would talk to the pitching coach, and he would talk to the backup catcher, and he would talk to the middle reliever. He'd find little things no one else was even looking for because they're all listening to Derek Jeter spew off his clichés from that night. That's really what makes great writing. It's finding the obscure, finding the small.
>
> (Jeff Pearlman, personal interview, 2017)

It's All about Relationships

A benefit of breaking off from the pack is the ability to dig a bit deeper with sources and establish relationships.

Tom Withers explains:

> As LeBron is talking, I go to Kevin Love and strike up a conversation. I lived in California for four years. He's a California kid. That gave us a connection. We talked about what we are watching on Netflix. If have the luxury of some time, we can get to know people on a different level than a journalist and an athlete.
>
> (Tom Withers, personal interview, 2018)

Bill Finley, who has covered sports for the *New York Times*, says mainstream athletes are often so managed by publicist they are almost on "autopilot":

> It's very hard to get good stuff out of them. The general reporter in the clubhouse or the locker room before a game or after a game is fortunate to just get a lot of clichés. The "we'll take it one game at a time" type of thing. The people that would tend to get something out of those premier athletes a less type athletes are the people that know them best—who have built up relationships with them over the years.
>
> (Bill Finley, personal interview, 2014)

Let Players Talk

The fact so many sports reporters were sports fans first can get in the way of good interview techniques. Too often, reporters will say to a player who just hit a home run, "It was the ninth inning, the bases were loaded, the pitch before that was a slider, then you fouled off a 2–2 fastball, so you were you sitting on the pitch." News consumers don't necessarily want the set up—they want to know what it feels like to hit a walk-off home-run, says Dan Plesac:

> Try, "What does it feel like when you are rounding first and you know it's a walk off?" What the people want at home they want a natural reaction out of player. They want to see a player get excited, they want to see a player laugh. You want to try to get more out of the guys so the fans feel like they know more than they did from just watching on TV.
> (Dan Plesac, personal interview, 2017)

Don't Get Discouraged

Accept that sometimes you are not going to catch that athlete or coach on the best day, and it's likely not you. Try and be empathetic and understanding. It will go a long way toward building a relationship.

The "Talk About" Curse

According to a 2015 article in Grantland, Marcus Mariota had six in one press conference before the 2015 National Championship. After winning that National Championship, Urban Meyer got four (Curtis, 2015).

They are "Talk about. . ." questions.

An example from a 2014 interview with Rory McIlroy:

Q: Could you talk about going into this year, there was a run of first time major champions, but this year all three of you guys have had major championships before. Just talk about how experience seems to pay more of a dividend this year.

McIlroy: It has, yeah. I mean, starting off with the Masters and Bubba, obviously, having won at Augusta before. He seems to have got that place figured out pretty well.

(Elbin, 2014)

The "talk about" question is a sports reporting stable, and one most reporters who hear it wish would fade, along with "walk us through," and "how big was it when . . .".

Figure 7.6 Steve Fox says his least favorite question in sports writing is "talk about . . ." He says if you want to know how someone feels about something, just ask them.

Source: Steve Fox

"The 'talk about question' is the worst," says Steve Fox, a longtime sports writer who teaches at University of Massachusetts. "If you want to know how someone feels about something, just ask them specifically how they feel" (personal interview, 2018).

It's Better to Ask No Question than a Stupid One

The examples of press conference questions that would have better been left unasked seems endless.

In the 2016 NCAA tournament, the 12th-seeded Yale Bulldogs beat the No. 5 Baylor Bears 79-75, and Baylor senior Taurean Prince was left to face the media and this question: "How did Yale out-rebound Baylor?"

Prince wasted no time in offering his response: "Um, you go up and grab the ball of the rim when it comes off, and you grab it with two hands, and you come down with it, and that's considered a rebound. So, they got more of those than we did" (NBC Sports, 2016).

And that was far from the worst question ever asked.

After the Los Angeles Clippers lost Game 5 of the 2016 NBA playoffs at home to the Utah Jazz, they were next headed for game six in Utah. Before they left, the Los Angeles Clipper's Chris Paul faced the media and this question: "Will the Clippers be back here Sunday playing a game 7?"

Paul furrows his brow in confusion and replies, "What?"

The reporter continues: "Your feeling about—your level of confidence that you'll be back here again."

Paul finally replies, "What you think? I'm on the team. What you want me to say? No, it's over? That's what you want to hear? Yes. Come on, man. You've been doing this long enough. Seriously, right?" (Joseph, 2017).

How about the reporter who asked San Antonio coach Greg Popovich after the Spurs Game 5 blowout of the Oklahoma City Thunder in the 2014 Western Conference Finals, "Five games, five blowouts. To us who don't really know the game, how do you explain that?

Popovich responds after a pause, "You're serious? You really think I can explain that?" (Freeman, 2014).

Kristaps Porzingis was short but sweet when faced with this question after the New York Knicks 2017 win over Indiana: "You're down 19 to the Pacers, you're down 11 heading into the fourth tonight in this game. Is there ever a point in which you don't think you can come back, and what's your mindset?"

His reply: "No" (Curtis, 2017).

Make the Calls

Athlete time is often of short supple, says Jeff Pearlman. He says a profile on some wide receiver at a university might net him only 10 minutes of face-to-face interview time, so that means his interviewing is just beginning:

> I'm finding who his friends are on campus, and I'm talking to them. Another thing is call his high school coach, find high school friends. If he has a Facebook page find his friends on Facebook, reach out to them. Be like, "I'm doing this profile on this guy; can I talk to you?" Social media has made my job and yours a million times easier because there's so much out there.
>
> High school coaches always have stories, and they always like talking. You talk to the high school coach and you say, "Hey, is there anyone from your team you'd recommend me talking to?" They're like, "Yeah, his best friend was Jimmy the wide receiver who's now a sophomore at Bucknell. Here's his number, give him a call." You basically build this amazing story around [the player].
>
> (Jeff Pearlman, personal interview, 2017)

Don't Take No for an Answer

In the course of managing player time, media relations personnel and sports information staff at universities may limit access to players. Don't be discouraged, says Jeff Pearlman, as there are often ways to reach athletes directly, in person and through social media accounts like Twitter and Instagram:

> I'm going to find the guy and I'm going to go talk to him. If he's a college student in the cafeteria one day I'm going to be like, "Hey, I really want to write this profile on you. Is there any way I can talk to you?" If you interview his friends and coaches, go back to him and you're like, "Look, I interviewed your high school coach, I interviewed your peewee coach, I interviewed your cousin Jim. I interviewed your best friend from high school. I really want to make this profile good. Can I please talk to you for a few extra minutes?"
>
> (Jeff Pearlman, personal interview, 2017)

References

Curtis, B. (2015). The Worst Question in Sports: What We Talk About When We Say "Talk About." January 22. Retrieved from http://grantland.com/the-trian gle/sports-media-press-conferences-nba-nfl-mlb-nhl-lebron-james-bill-belichick/

Curtis, C. (2017). Kristaps Porzingis Had the Best Postgame Response. November 8. Retrieved June 18, 2018, from www.usatoday.com/story/sports/ftw/2017/ 11/08/kristaps-porzingis-had-the-best-postgame-response-to-question-about-knicks-comeback-win/107461726/

Davies, S. (2018). LeBron James Sends Best Wishes to Cleveland Browns in NFL Draft. April 25. Retrieved June 20, 2018, from https://lebronwire.usatoday. com/2018/04/25/lebron-james-wishes-best-to-cleveland-browns-future-no-1-pick-in-nfl-draft/

Elbin, K. (2014). 2014 PGA Championship Interview With: Rory McIlroy. August 4. Retrieved June 20, 2018, from www.pga.com/pgachampionship/interviews/ tuesday/2014-pga-championship-rory-mcilroy.

Freeman, E. (2014). Gregg Popovich Won't Answer Reporter's Question after Game 5 Win. May 14. Retrieved June 18, 2018, from https://sports.yahoo.com/ gregg-popovich-won-t-answer-reporter-s-question-after-game-5-win—video-045051212.html?y20=1.

James, L. (2017). Tweet: U bum @StephenCurry30 Already Said He Ain't Going! So Therefore Ain't No Invite. Going to White House Was a Great Honor until You Showed Up! September 23. Retrieved June 20, 2018, from https://twitter. com/kingjames/status/911610455877021697?lang=en.

Joseph, A. (2017). Chris Paul Couldn't Hold Back His Disbelief at a Reporter's Ridiculous Question. April 26. Retrieved June 20, 2018, from https://ftw.usato day.com/2017/04/chris-paul-press-conference-question-reporter-clippers-vs-jazz-nba-playoffs.

NBC Sports. (2016). Baylor's Taurean Prince Explains What a Rebound Is to Reporter. March 18. Retrieved June 20, 2018, from www.nbcsports.com/video/baylors-taurean-prince-explains-what-rebound-reporter.

Petchesky, B. (2013). We Remind All Big Ten Reporters That Asking For Coach's Autograph Is Not Acceptable (Update: Ed Responds). June 17. Retrieved June 20, 2018, from https://deadspin.com/5826605/we-remind-all-big-ten-reporters-that-asking-for-coachs-autograph-is-not-acceptable.

Shelton, R. (Director). (1988). *Bull Durham*. Motion picture. United States: Orion Pictures.

8 Speeches, Press Conference and Meetings, Oh My

For many journalistic stories, information will come from on-the-spot or pre-planned one-on-one interviews. But in other articles, it might come in other pre-set formats, such as speeches, press conference and meetings.

In truth, these are not exactly interviews, but they do involve many of the skills we have developed for interviewing, including:

* observation;
* accurate chronicling of information; and
* identifying the order information must be presented to readers.

Let's look at how to handle some of these situations that go off the beaten interviewing path.

Press Conferences

Press conferences can be both the easiest and hardest reporting you can do. They are set in a finite time and space with no coordination on your part. That's the good news. The bad news is you are extremely limited in the questions you can ask. All those questions are also asked in front of every other journalist interested in the topic.

Unlike sports, in which a press conference provides subject availability, a press conference is usually intended to convey a set agenda of information. The main subject will make an announcement and then invite questions from those who have gathered. They determine the subject, location and duration, as well as how many questions they may be willing to take.

To be successful at a press conference, you need to be focused on your question and—I beg of you—not waste time asking one of the countless closed-ended, leading or lazy questions we hear during every televised press event.

As Charlie Leerhsen says, if you watch the Oscars or the Kentucky Derby, invariable someone will ask: "How excited were you when such

Figure 8.1 Press conferences attract all forms of media to have access to information being released, but it's the questions asked after the event that might make your story stand out.

Source: Creative Commons/Pxhere

and such happen, or how nervous were you?" He calls such inquiries "horrible questions" and "a waste of a great opportunity":

> You're talking to somebody who's in a very important position at the moment, and what you're doing is assigning the emotion yourself. The only possible answers to those things are a whole lot of nothing. If someone's going to really give you an interesting answer to that question they have to kind of take the question and change it anyway. It's better to talk about how they felt as they were going to kick that field goal or talk about they felt as they sat in the audience waiting.
>
> (Charlie Leerhsen, personal interview, 2014)

Here are some press conference tips:

1 **Do some research.** Just like more conventional interviews, research into the source or the topic of the press conference will help you develop questions. Come prepared with questions you might want to ask. It is conceivable some questions may not be on the intended topic of the press conference organizer. Once someone is in front of you, your topics are fair game, although they may not answer them.

2 **Get close.** Where you sit in a press conference can help you get noticed when it comes time for questions, but most important is that you get a clear and accurate recording of what is being said. Instead of holding your phone or recorder, place it (turned on) on the podium to pick up the speaker's voice. You may also pick up side comments not intended for the general public. If the podium is not available, and you are far from the source, look for the closest speaker and record your audio from there

3 **Don't be intimidated.** It is scary and intimidating to ask questions at a press conference. You are on the spot in front of countless other people who are all waiting for you to finish so they can get their own question addressed. You have the same rights as all the others, and you have been trained to ask good questions. Have faith in your abilities and showcase them well.

4 **Bring good questions with you.** To maximize exposure and limit embarrassment, do not be the person that asks the question all others think is insignificant. Remember our game of chess? Ask the question in your head before you ask it aloud and envision how it may be answered. If the answer is what you need, ask it. If not, think how to rephrase it. You need to figure out what information you need to know and be prepared to ask your question as succinctly as possible.

5 **Don't be surprised if someone else asks your questions.** Come equipped with as many good questions as you can, and ask your best question first. If someone else asks it first, ask your next best question. Get your issues as addressed.

6 **Don't rely on others to ask your questions.** Many reporters have been to numerous press conferences with the lurker—the one who sits back and lets others do the heavy lifting of developing and asking questions. Don't be that reporter. Be proactive and aggressive!

7 **Don't accept the brush off.** Those who call press conferences have an agenda, and they will do all they can to stick to their own message. You may ask a question that elicits a response completely off topic. Keep pushing for the answers you need.

8 **Cut through the jargon.** That agenda comes with its own lexicon, and that is not the lexicon that serves your readers. Cut through government-speak or trending terms and just break out for the readers what they need and want to know in terms they understand.

9 **You will get blown off at some point. Live with it.** The likelihood is there, especially at high-level reporting (government, statehouse, college or pro sports, etc.) that you will, at some point, get a curt or hostile answer to a question or get blown off completely (and publicly). Steel yourself for this prospect, and learn to live with it. Come back. Press them to answer your question or figure out a follow-up.

10 **Get it right.** Make sure to get the name of all the people who speak, as well as the spellings, before you leave the press conference.

Concurrently, remember that every other reporter in the room heard (and likely recorded) exactly what you did. Make sure you have chronicled the event accurately, or it will be extremely obvious when your article comes out and it differs from other accounts.

11. **Stick around.** The communal nature of press conferences means getting an exclusive story is tough, but your questions and the angle you pick for the story will help you craft a piece that may be different from all other coverage. For that reason, don't rush out when the event is over. You can often approach the subject and ask questions after the event, out of earshot of other reporters to strive for more originality in your coverage.

Meetings and Speeches

On the surface, meetings and speeches would seem the opposite of interviews. You are there to collect and report on information provided by others without asking questions. Sitting through these sessions and accurately weeding through and reporting on what is said, however, is only the first step in this process.

Public meetings are where the government and public come in contact with one another, and people can see the government do its business. Usually there is time offered for the public to speak or question, but this is not the time for reporters to ask questions. Instead, pay attention to what community members may find important. Post-meeting and post-speech are the ideal times to grab elected officials and speakers. They are already in front of you and should be able to provide immediate information on the topics.

Figure 8.2 Community members join at public meetings to hear from elected officials and understand workings of government. Although the meeting itself is not the time for questions, it's a great place to grab officials and citizens to talk about issues brought up.

Source: Creative Commons/FEMA

Question development comes as the meeting or speech is being conducted and your approach comes immediately after its conclusion. Introduce yourself and say you have a few follow-up questions. Then begin asking.

Make sure you are ready to take notes accurately, and recognize that you may have a limited amount of time. Always get contact information for the person with whom you speak and let them know you may be following up if you have more questions. Even if you may not need them again for this story, chances are you will need them again in the future.

Another interview facet of meetings and speeches comes from audience engagement of the topic. Getting comments from members of the public who attended a meeting and have a vested interest in a community topic could help provide context. Reflections from those who experience the speech will help readers see the significance of the event and the topic. When covering a campaign speech, questions may surround what the subject thinks about the candidate after the speech, likelihood of voting for that candidate and their views on the key topics discussed.

In a commencement speech, audience questions might revolve around what graduates thought about the message, and how and why it resonated with those leaving college.

A benefit of speeches is often a copy will be made available before the event, which will help reporters get a sense of the key focus areas. That does not mean, however, that the speech will follow that script exactly, so attendance and focus are still important.

9 Interviewing across Media

As an advocate and practitioner of active learning, I like to send students out to conduct their first audio or video interviews as a low-stakes assessment. They receive little instruction and get full points for participating. The goal is to let them make mistakes and then learn from those mistakes, so they are less likely to make them again.

What do we see print-focused reporters do from an electronic interview standpoint? They shoot audio or video that is:

- too far away, so audio is too low;
- in a location with much noise and clamor, like a student union, or outside on a windy day;
- has camera or recorder motion so much it distorts audio or makes viewer nauseous; and
- interrupted by the interviewer with verbal fillers like, "uh huh," "I know," etc., which comprises sound bite potential.

"In [audio] you are looking for a complete answer," says long-time sports radio reporter Lori Schmidt:

> [A print reporter] may interject if they aren't getting the answer they are looking for. You can't interrupt a sound bite in radio. You have to let them continue—which has its own advantages. Print writers are very, very specific. In radio, you have so little time, you can't ask about this or that third-down play. We get to ask questions more big picture questions, more zoomed out on the situation.
>
> (Lori Schmidt, personal interview, 2018)

Much about the fundamentals of interviewing will remain the same across media platforms, including:

- Research.
- Question development—open-ended is king!
- Source cultivation.
- Telling stories of source.

Figure 9.1 Sound, background and proximity to the source are all factors in a successful video interview.

Source: Creative Commons/Hadi

But much about interviewing across media is different, including:

- Tools we use.
- How we ask questions.
- Interview locations.

Equipment

We are not going to cover the specific equipment you will need for video or audio reporting, but there are some basic needs to understand. While a pad and pencil, or even a cheap recorder, will serve an interview where words are produced to be filtered through your hand, a multimedia interview has to stand on its own.

If it's audio, that means you will need an external microphone and recording equipment to provide a high-quality recording, as well as earphones for you to hear what the subject is saying—and how it is coming across through the equipment.

For video, you will need a camera—motion or high-quality still camera that also captures HD video, as well as ports for your external microphone and earphones. Invest in either a small boom mike or a lavalier you can attach to your subject.

The best video does not come from a camera alone, though. A tripod will stabilize your shot and give you flexibility (so you are not stuck behind the camera).

Digital technology has never been easier, and there are countless journalists who use their iPhones or iPads for audio and video recording. Both are great resources, but you may want more versatility in terms of zoom and exposures.

If you are using the iPhone or iPad, invest in a holder and tripod and apps that will expand the camera's capabilities. You can also use the microphone/earphone that comes with the iPhone as a microphone.

Questions and Answers

While the fact that we ask questions remains constant across media, the way we ask is what changes. Open-ended questions produce the most engaging and revealing answers. You need to be ready with solid follow-up questions, so listening is key.

"We ask questions that are more big picture, more zoomed out on the situation," says Lori Schmidt. "You want it to be open-ended enough to get a good answer and want it to be a question you are interested in the answer" (personal interview, 2018).

Single subject questions are ideal for print, but we may ask two-part questions in media to allow greater length in response.

Another challenge is when your subject hears your question and starts answering from that point—great for you two, but not so much if your viewers have no idea what was the question:

> QUESTION: "How long have you been working at the company and what brought you here?"
>
> ANSWER: "Thirty years. It was my first job out of college and I just never left."

In print, you could paraphrase your question to give context and say:

> "John Smith had been working at the company for the past 30 years. "It was my first job out of college, and I just never left," he said.

In video, however, the answer is almost useless. Try asking your subject to repeat your question in their answer:

> "I've been working for this company for 30 years. It was my first job out of college and I just never left."

Prompting

Another of the most crucial aspects of a conversation (i.e., interview) is how we prompt others ("Really?" "I see." "That's interesting.") With media, you have to be a lot quieter because, guess what, the camera now picks up your comments for all the world to hear.

To show your subject you are listening, practice:

- Nodding.
- Smiling and nodding.
- Raising your eyebrows and nodding.
- Leaning forward in your chair.
- Laughing without making sound.

Yes, you will at first feel a bit dorky. It's OK. Those interruptions you can get away with sometimes in print (even though they are not helpful) will be an interview killer in video or audio. You will simply not be able to use what could be a good quote.

Box 9.1 Greasing the Conversation

There are two main types of phrase, words and expressions that keep conversations, and therefore interviews, going—one for the source and one for the interviewer.

- **Source**: Filler words, such as "um", "you know" and "like".

People use them to transition between thoughts, without having to stop talking, allowing their part of the conversation top continue. When quoting sources, you can remove these filler words without compromising the verbatim requirement.

- **Interviewer:** Indirect words of encouragement, such as "uh huh," "really," "interesting," and "I hear what you are saying."

Note these are not words of agreement, per se. If you are interviewing a tanning bed worker for a story on the benefits vs. dangers of tanning, responding, "Oh my gosh, I just love to tan, too!" just compromised your objectivity. Instead, for someone raving about the perks of tanning, you can say, "How interesting. I totally hear what you are saying."

The exception to these comments are video and audio interviews, where your own interjections intended to keep the conversation

---

going will actually doom your soundbites, as you will interrupt your source's words.

In this case, we practice silent affirmations, such as nodding your head, laughing silently, leaning in and even with a hand motion encouraging them to continue.

Environment

Noisy print interview locations mean you may have trouble transcribing your notes. A noisy location for video or audio often makes it useless. Try to get sources to as quiet as spot as is possible, recognizing that news breaks where it breaks and you have to do the best you can in those circumstances. But it you are setting up a longer interview on camera, find a quiet spot with a neutral background, where your subject can be comfortable.

Having your subject sit down can make them quite comfortable, but beware of the swivel chair. Someone sitting in a chair that moves will very often make the chair move. And everyone on the video will see it.

Sound is a funny thing. You often don't hear the beeping of a truck backing up or a dumpster being emptied, or even the overhead fan in a room until it's on your recording. Really listen to what is going on around you, and record about one minute of just the neutral sounds in the room to later provide sound breaks in your recording if you need them.

In addition, that lavalier mic you positioned on a source's left lapel? Make sure you position the source to talk in that direction—and keep talking in that direction. A mouth that moves away and toward a microphone is a sound editor's nightmare!

Camera Position

Video is shot in wide, medium and tight sequences, but interviews need to be shot close so you can see "the whites of their eyes," to coin a term from Old Westerns. Facial expression is a key part of an interview, so get close up, and frame so your source is looking into the shot (on the mid right side looking left into the frame). Avoid having sources talk directly into the camera so the viewer feels part of the conversation but not the direct focus.

Think about the perspective of height. Are you shooting down on the subject? Are you shooting up? Eye level puts us all on equal ground.

Pay Attention to the Background

Video bombers, sudden loud noises, people crossing behind or in front of your subject will all impact your video interview. Make sure there is not too much happening in the background that might detract from your own interview.

Figure 9.2 Capturing a press conference with an iPad allows recording of audio for an article and vide to augment the piece.

Source: Nicole Kraft

A Gentle Reminder

While recording, you can remind your source what the story is about to get the conversation started to orient the interview and ensure they know they are being recorded,

"Thanks for agreeing to talk. As you might recall, we are doing a video (or audio broadcast) on whether the city remove these horseshoe pits to replace with a basketball court. You are a member of the horseshoe club. I wanted to talk to you about your thoughts on this plan."

Nice to Meet You

Ask your subject to introduce himself or herself, as well as share some background information. Also ask them to spell it. You can get a sound level and possibly use the introduction in the story.

Podcasting

The kind of interview you do is very much related to what you what your final product to be.

(Tara Boyle, personal interview, 2018)

Figure 9.3 Radio has long been an important source of news and information.
Source: Creative Commons/USAID

In a 2004 article in *The Guardian*, Ben Hammersely noted the rise of MP3 players, like Apple's iPod, combined with cheap or free audio production software, added to the freedom of internet publishing and broadcasting led to a "new boom in amateur radio" (Hammersley, 2004).

Among the names he suggested for this new medium, one stuck: podcasting.

"Podcasting is just good radio on steroids," says Jo Ingles of Ohio Public Radio:

> I can choose what I listen to. If you listen to NPR, you may have to hear about archeology or other subjects that don't interest you. With a podcast, you know what you are getting. It's presented in a way that is more conversational. It appeals to more people who wouldn't listen to radio, which they make think is stuffy.
>
> (Jo Ingles, personal interview, 2018)

Tara Boyle, supervising producer of the successful NPR podcast *Hidden Brain*, hosted by Shankar Vedantam, says podcasts are a union of preferences and predilections of audio producers, matching the convenience and desire of listeners to have things on demand:

> For a lot of good stories it feel like a person is taking you by the hand and giving you a guided journey. When people listened to old-time radio, they heard those stories. We are not reinventing the wheel. We are

keeping with the oral traditions of radio and how we tell stories for the ear.

(Tara Boyle, personal interview, 2018)

For a strong podcast, interviewers must be clear who is the audience and how does this source fit that audience or a specific topic or segment. Podcasting a personalized listening experience, and that connection to the listener is what keeps people coming back episode after episode.

To lead your audience on that journey, conduct expensive research into your subject and flush out the intersection between subject and audience.

We created a podcast called *Student Slant* as part of our Ohio State journalism classes, to provide the insider view of student journalism—how it gets done and what student journalists need to know about the real world of reporting. As part of the show, students have interviewed some incredible guests, including Phil Mattingly of CNN, Gerrick Kennedy of the *Los Angeles Times* and Phillip Bump of the *Washington Post*. These people have incredible stories and examples to share, but what connects them all is they are alums of Ohio State, so we need to ensure our podcasts convers their time on campus, and what they learned through their journey that might benefit current students.

Figure 9.4 Shankar Vedantam interviews Nobel Prize Winner Daniel Kahneman in March 2018.
Source: Eric Lee/NPR

That means formulating the right questions and creating a narrative arc that allows for us to cover the narrative that will most appeal to our listeners.

Tara Boyle says the key to podcasting interviewing is to focus on that sense of intimacy in a conversational interview and bring it to subject-based dialogue, without letting it drone on "because you love sound of your voice."

"When we are approaching an interview we are being ruthless, and cutting, cutting, cutting," she says. "We focus on language and turn of phrase and make writing as crisp as possible" (personal interview, 2018).

Pre-planning of questions will help achieve that crispness, but to maximize potential for a good interview to become great, be flexible enough to build rapport and make the subject feel relaxed—like they are conversing among friends.

According to Boyle, 60 percent of podcast work happens on the front end, understanding what story you want to tell, and developing the questions that will drive the dialogue with purpose.

"We talk a lot about pacing and how to get it right," she says. "We are trying to unfold a story slowly and deliberately."

Reference

Hammersley, B. (2004). Why Online Radio is Booming. February 12. Retrieved June 20, 2018, from www.theguardian.com/media/2004/feb/12/broadcasting.digitalmedia.

10 Ethics of Interviewing

Journalism is filled with ethical challenges, and some of the most common start on our path to interviewing.

Can I interview my family, friends and people I know?

The short answer for news is no, no and sometimes. The short answer for magazine features is maybe, sometimes and sometimes. Policies on this can differ with the publication. It is imperative you ask your editor before you interview someone who may cross the line.

The goal is to maintain your professionalism and stay above any perception of impropriety. Can you really write objectively on your father or your sister? Probably not. How about a friend? If you are truly honest, will they still be your friend and might that impact how you write? Someone you have met or know to have a good story? That may be less problematic.

With social media, we have "friends" where we never did before and are "linked to" or "following" people we may have never met. That has blurred the lines, but not the intention of the ethical consideration. The perception of impropriety is impropriety. If a reader or viewer thinks you were biased due to your relationship with this source, then you were.

Your Interview Subject Asks to See Your Questions Ahead of Time.

What do you do?

Your options are:

1 Send them all.
2 Send a few of them.
3 Send some topics but not the exact questions.
4 Don't send anything.

There is nothing unethical about sending questions. Some will say that it helps sources prepare for the interview ahead of time. Others, however, say it gives them time to rehearse and the answers do not sound natural or spontaneous. Both answers are accurate, and the more sensitive the subject matter, the less likely you may want your subject to know you will be talking about it.

I often tell sources the subject we will be discussing to get them thinking ahead, and maybe a few topical highlights, but I never send questions—in part because my questions change so much depending on the direction of the interview. And I do want to surprise them into giving spontaneous answers.

I also love when someone who has been interviewed a lot says, "That's a good question; I haven't been asked that before." You can't get that if they already have the questions!

A bigger debate ensues around the idea of providing a copy of an article to a subject before it is published. Most publications are staunchly against this, as it leaves open the possibility for manipulation of the content. Other publications say it ensures accuracy. Be sure to check with an editor before you show a subject an article.

Box 10.1 Code of Ethics

The Society of Professional Journalists sets the standard of media ethics through its Code of Ethics, and many of them apply specifically to the gathering of information through interviews. They include:

- Take responsibility for the accuracy of their work. Verify information before releasing it. Use original sources whenever possible.
- Identify sources clearly. The public is entitled to as much information as possible to judge the reliability and motivations of sources.
- Consider sources' motives before promising anonymity. Reserve anonymity for sources who may face danger, retribution or other harm, and have information that cannot be obtained elsewhere. Explain why anonymity was granted.
- Diligently seek subjects of news coverage to allow them to respond to criticism or allegations of wrongdoing.
- Support the open and civil exchange of views, even views they find repugnant.
- Boldly tell the story of the diversity and magnitude of the human experience. Seek sources whose voices we seldom hear.
- Never deliberately distort facts or context, including visual information. Clearly label illustrations and re-enactments.
- Never plagiarize. Always attribute.

Source: Society of Professional Journalists (n.d.)

Your interview was over, but you left the recorder on by accident, and your source gave you the best quotes of the entire session. Can you use them?

Absolutely! Often you get the most revealing or intimate comments when a subject feels more relaxed and out of the spotlight. If they don't say "off the record," it's all fair.

Don't rely on leaving the recorder on by accident—do it as a matter of course.

You are interviewing someone whose views are completely opposite to your own. How do you make sure you don't let it show?

Let your natural curiosity take over and put your own views aside for the time being. Just as we don't want to taint an interview by agreeing with a subject we admire, we don't want to be confrontational to a source we do not like or agree with. But we do want to ask the questions that readers want answered, so we certainly don't give people a pass on controversial topics.

Let's say you are a dog lover and the city you cover is pondering a restrictive leash law. Remember that your primary concern is finding out what the readers want to know, and you will have readers on both sides of the topic. You plan to interview a city councilman who pushed the law.

Some questions you may want to consider for this source:

- What is the motivation behind the new leash law?
- What impact will it have on residents?
- What are the benefits for the city with this new law?
- Walk me through the complaints you have received that led to this leash law.
- There are clearly two passionate sides to this issue. How do you respond to those who feel the city has let them and their pets down with this law?
- What options do owners have who want their pets to have time and space off leash?

Even when you may appear confrontational, it is fact supported.

How do you handle interviewing children and unsophisticated sources?

This became a major issue in December 2012 after the Sandy Hook Elementary School shooting, when reporters converged on Newtown, Connecticut, and interviewed elementary age kids after their classmates had been killed. Children—especially the ones who are as young as those at Sandy Hook—ethically cannot agree to be interviewed, and it is unethical to seek interviews with them without their parents' permission.

Figure 10.1 Reporters are encouraged to seek sources through social media, but this tweet received much backlash, as it was considered insensitive.

Source: Twitter

As John Temple of the *Washington Post* wrote:

> Young children aren't able to understand what a reporter is or does and what the ramifications of their words are. So you don't interview a child, and certainly not an elementary school child, without permission.
>
> (Farhi, 2012)

A major tenant of journalism ethics is do no harm, so avoid putting any interview subjects—especially kids—through more trauma. Kids need to be old enough to understand the ramifications of their statements to be ethically interviewed. Elementary-school-age kids should always have parental permission for interviews, although middle- and high school-age kids have more latitude. The focus on interviewing high school students shifted with the Marjory Stoneman Douglas school shooting on February 14, 2018, as the student body became the most outspoken sources.

We also have a responsibility to protect other sources that have little media experience and may be in a vulnerable position. Victims and witnesses of crimes, even when they are adults, have been thrust into a spotlight they did not seek, and we need to treat them fairly in the quest for information.

The same can be true of people who are simply attending an event or have a view on a subject on which you are writing—without the involvement of any controversy. Those inexperienced with the media have little idea what it means to have their words written down verbatim and published—think about how many times you have said in the heat of excitement of a moment something that was an embellishment or exaggeration.

Would you really want such a statement printed?

Box 10.2 Victim Interviews

Interviewing victims of crimes and disasters is never easy, and it requires special ethical considerations. The key in these interviews is compassion without judgment. Acknowledge this may be a tough time, and your job is to fairly and accurately report what happened.

Impress upon your interview subjects that you wish to simply report the facts; offer victims the opportunity to tell their side of the story, or to share with the public something that makes their loved ones more than just a name on a police report.

"Be a good guy," says Randy Ludlow of the *Columbus Dispatch*. "Don't come across as the brass tacks, hard-nosed reporter. You have to have empathy for people, especially when they deal with loss of a loved one—murder, soldier killed. You have to be gentle."

Holly Zachariah of the *Columbus Dispatch* has covered her share of emotionally charged stories and interviewed victims "on the worst day of their lives." She says she often starts by explaining why she is there, what story she is seeking to write or report, and why it is important for sources to speak to her.

Key to covering crime is not to revictimize subjects, as is evidenced by the Society of Professional Journalists Code of Ethics, which states, "Minimize harm," and offers these guidelines:

- Balance the public's need for information against potential harm or discomfort. Pursuit of the news is not a license for arrogance or undue intrusiveness.
- Show compassion for those who may be affected by news coverage. Use heightened sensitivity when dealing with juveniles, victims of sex crimes, and sources or subjects who are inexperienced or unable

to give consent. Consider cultural differences in approach and treatment.

- Recognize that legal access to information differs from an ethical justification to publish or broadcast.
- Realize that private people have a greater right to control information about themselves than public figures and others who seek power, influence or attention. Weigh the consequences of publishing or broadcasting personal information.
- Avoid pandering to lurid curiosity, even if others do.
- Balance a suspect's right to a fair trial with the public's right to know. Consider the implications of identifying criminal suspects before they face legal charges.
- Consider the long-term implications of the extended reach and permanence of publication. Provide updated and more complete information as appropriate.

Language is a primary consideration when interviewing those who have suffered crime or tragedy. Phrases like, "How do you feel?" or, worse, "I know how you feel," will quickly drive a wedge between you and your interview subject.

Trust is a key facet of the relationship when interviewing crime victims. Your manner and your first words will tell the other person whether he should trust you and how sincere you are. Those first impressions may decide whether you are ever again able to interview that person.

A tip sheet from the Dart Center for Journalism and Trauma for college media advisors, editors and student journalists, entitled "Covering Breaking News: Interviewing Victims and Survivors," offers tips to minimize harm to subjects. It includes:

- Doing research before going out into the field to know what happened and how it has impacted people in the vicinity.
- Discuss with an editor a plan for news gathering and interviewing.
- Ensuring the area is clear and safe.
- Be ready for the long haul by bringing basic supplies (e.g. water, rain gear, hat, extra batteries, etc.) with you in case you are posted to a spot for hours.
- Be transparent, calm and soft-spoken when approaching sources, including identify who you are, what organization you represent, what will happen with the information you collect from the

interview, how it might be used in the story and when it will appear in publication.

- Telling sources why you want to talk with them. If they are open to an interview, then proceed. If not, then leave your contact information with them and ask them to contact you anytime if they would like to talk. If they are not interested in talking, or willing to speak on the record, there will be another opportunity to find another source.
- Let the interview subject have some control. People who have undergone a traumatic situation often seek ways to regain control in their lives. One way to honor this is to give them a chance to make some decisions in the interview process – for example, where they would like to sit and what photos or images they would prefer that you to use. You might also let them to tell you when they want to stop or take a break.
- Be sincere when meeting with victims and survivors. Don't patronize. Don't ask "How do you feel?" or say "I know how you feel," – because in most cases nobody truly knows what somebody else is going through. Be supportive in the way you communicate.
- Consider empathic interviewing. Empathy is the capacity to participate in another's sensations, feelings, thoughts, and movements. Using specific words can make a difference in the interview and in how your interview subject responds. The premise of empathic interviewing shows the source your interest, attentiveness and care in telling their story. Such responses include:

  - "So what you're saying is ..."
  - "From what you're saying, I can see how you would be ..."
  - "You must be ..."

- Interview details can be hazy. Interview subjects may experience memory loss, and sources may not remember all of the details of what happened. Don't pressure them to remember. It may come in due time. Corroborate information with other sources as you would for any kind of news story.

Holly Zachariah is known for her emotional connection to stories, a trait she feels helps her connect better with sources—especially those facing trauma. She cited a mentor, the late *Columbus Dispatch* columnist Mike Harden, who told her, "Only heart lasts." Zachariah says that guides her in everything she does.

"It doesn't mean I can't be an investigative reporter and it doesn't mean I can't be a hard-hitting reporter but it means I never lose sight of the fact that these people are humans," she says. "If I'm telling hard news you still have to be mindful."

She cites the example of a triple murderer she interviewed in prison. His children had done nothing wrong; demonizing him in print would do nothing to foster understanding of his crimes.

"It doesn't mean I have to change the story or alter it in any way of course but it means I come at it thinking I don't want to do unnecessary harm," she says. "I don't want to be over-the-top about him. He's evil enough. I don't need to make him into a worse character, so you have to balance it."

Zachariah admits she is the reporter who gets teased for crying in the back of the courtroom or pulling out tissues at an interview. She feels no shame and said she believes it makes her a better reporter. But she never loses sight of the reporter relationship:

> I'm here to tell your story, and we need to remember that. It is a balance, and it and it weighs heavy on my mind and the mind of any good journalist. A lot of your stories are very tragic stories they're full of emotion do you feel like you're one emotional stance on it you just mentioned that you're the reporter that cries in a courtroom do you think you're almost capturing your own emotion through writing that story that's a great question and I check myself every day.
>
> The really the big thing is don't be a jerk. To be a good reporter, you have to be a good person. I think we should all just be good humans we should get up morning thinking, "How can I be better than I was yesterday?" We should strive to not be a jerk. That translates into making you a better reporter.

Sources: Dart Center (2015); Society of Professional Journalists (n.d.); Randy Ludlow, personal interview, 2014; Holly Zachariah, personal interview, 2018

A source said they will comment on impropriety in the school district, but only if you don't use his or her name?

Most reporters and news agencies agree that for a story to use unnamed sources, it should be of overwhelming public concern and there must be no other way to get the essential information on the record. Consider what the use of an unnamed source mean to the actual and perceived authenticity of the story and if readers or viewers will evaluate the same information if they knew the name and motivations of the source.

A study by Jonathan Peters, Genelle Belmas and Piotr Bobkowski of the University of Kansas in 2017 revealed that 40 states and the District of Columbia recognize "a reporter's privilege either in statutory form or in a functionally equivalent rule of evidence adopted by the state supreme court." The study also showed that nine of the remaining 10 states recognized the privilege through common law—with the exception of Wyoming (Peters, Belmas & Bobkowski, 2017).

But that protection does not extend into the federal realm, so consider whether the story and source are significant enough you are willing to go to jail rather than reveal his or her name (see more on unnamed sources in Chapter 2).

This quote would be perfect if I just added a word here or there, or changed this around a little. That wouldn't be a problem—right? Or couldn't I just add one little quote. It sounds just like something the person I interviewed would say—and it would be perfect for this piece.

Just about every young journalist has been tempted—on deadline or just by laziness—to do just this, but it is one of the clearest and simplest rules in journalism: Do not do it.

Making up quotes is fabrication. You will be fired.

Changing quotes is fabrication. You will be fired.

A quote is verbatim, with the only allowable changes being the removal of verbal lubricants—"like," "you know," etc. If you need to take out a piece and tighten the quote, us ellipses (. . .) to show something has been taken out—and only do this if the meaning is maintained. If the quote is really unusable verbatim, but the sentiment is clear and needed, paraphrase.

Box 10.1 "It's about Truth and Facts"

The following is an article (written by myself) that initially appeared in the Summer 2017 newsletter for the Media Ethics Division of the Association of Educators in Journalism and Mass Communication.

Therese Apel, who describes herself on Twitter as the "crime/breaking/mayhem reporter" for Mississippi's *Clarion-Ledger*, got the call May 31 at 3 a.m. An officer was down in Lincoln County and three other people may be dead.

Apel knew Lincoln, and she knew its police force, having served the community as both a reporter and a volunteer firefighter. She grabbed her camera and ran. The officer dead was Deputy William Dur, with whom Apel had worked for years.

And the story got worse as night became day. The death toll was actually eight people. The suspect, Willie Corey Godbolt, was on the loose. Apel was on the run again when a second call came through the police radio—Godbolt had been found and opened fire.

Figure 10.2 Theresa Apel has built such a strong relationship with law enforcement that they provide her with unequaled access to crime scenes and suspects.

Source: Theresa Apel

By the time she arrived, Godbolt was in custody with a gunshot wound to his arm. He had been read his Miranda rights. She originally thought he might be dead, but then he started to move. She started to roll her camera, capturing the scene of controlled chaos. She inched her way closer to Godbolt, now seated on the roadway beside a plain-clothed police officer, his left arm bandaged, feet splayed out before him, his arms handcuffed behind his back.

And as he looked into her camera lens, he began to talk. "My pain wasn't designed for him," Godbolt said, speaking into a camera about Dur. "He was just there."

Godbolt explained he had gone to his in-laws to talk about his children. At some point neighbors called police, and the deputy arrived. Four people were left dead at that scene. The video lasts 1:10, and in it the two have a quiet and direct conversation, without police interest or input. The only interjection is the beep of an ambulance backing up.

Apel asked, "So, what's next for you?"

"Death," Godbolt replied. "My intention was to have [them] kill me. I ran out of bullets."

Her reply: "It's a good thing they showed mercy."

"Suicide by cop was my intention," he continued. "I ain't fit to live, not after what I done. Not in y'all eyes. Not in nobody's eyes. But God. He forgives you for everything."

Godbolt then looks off to his left, and the video ends.

It's every reporter's dream to be one-on-one with a source that gives quotes that are too good to make up. While reporters often wait hours or days for police to provide info readers are clamoring to know —what happened and why—almost never does a murder suspect personally provide the information. Except it happened to Apel.

In the days after posting the video, Apel faced her share of critics. There are those who feel she gave a suspected killer a right of expression he did not deserve. Others say the attention put the focus on the killer rather than those killed. Even the Society of Professional Journalists Code of Ethics, in the section entitled, "Minimize Harm," lists coverage considerations that might apply to such a scenario, including:

- Recognize that legal access to information differs from an ethical justification to publish or broadcast.
- Avoid pandering to lurid curiosity, even if others do. Following a Mississippi shooting, a reporter videotapes the suspect's confession while he was handcuffed on the side of the road. Ethical issues? You bet.
- Balance a suspect's right to a fair trial with the public's right to know. Consider the implications of identifying criminal suspects before they face legal charges.

I spoke with Apel just hours after she covered the funeral of Dur, including a live Facebook stream. She was open in retelling the story, and she admitted that if not the trust she had built through years as a police reporter—and her own experiences as a first responder— she would likely never have had such access.

She knows her level of access made some uncomfortable and brought up questions of objectivity or the motivations behind broadcasting something as controversial as a confession just hours after a murder spree. She stands firmly behind her reporting.

"I'm not worried about prejudicing anybody," she said. "He was not under duress ... it came straight from his mouth. Everyone here knew I was a reporter. I was standing there when he was Mirandized, and he continued to talk. That's why I stayed where I was. I wanted it all on tape. The more he talks the better.

"I knew this is my job, and there is nobody else in the world who can do this right here."

Apel said the real lesson is to see and understand the rapport reporters can build with agencies that allow such a level of trust and respect. It takes a reporter who understands boundaries, and is fair and accurate in reporting the news.

Covering police and crime is tricky, especially amid the current polarization between community and police. The role of the media could not be more important, Apel said. But she fears too few young journalists see coverage in black and white, right and wrong, media and authorities. They may not be comfortable building the relationships that matter for news that involves life and death.

"If we are all doing the right thing, we are working toward the greater good for the world," she said. "If we are all on the same page, it's about truth and facts and things you can't manipulate."

Source: reprinted with permission of the Association of Educators in Journalism and Mass Communication

The Ethics of Dating Sources

It is not uncommon to date people you meet at work, which leaves reporters and sources vulnerable for relationships to develop. Among the most famous such relationships may be that of Connie Schultz, who met and married Sherrod Brown in 2004 while a columnist for the *Cleveland Plain Dealer*. She took a leave of absence during Brown's successful 2006 campaign for U.S. Senate, and resigned in 2011 during Brown's re-election bid. She told colleagues in an email:

> In recent weeks, it has become painfully clear that my independence, professionally and personally, is possible only if I'm no longer writing for the newspaper that covers my husband's senate race on a daily basis. It's time for me to move on.
>
> (Cano, 2011)

The issue came to prominence again in 2018 when Allie Watkins of the *New York Times* had an affair with James Wolfe, senior aide to the Senate Intelligence Committee, which resulted in a federal investigation and Wolfe's arrest for lying to investigators (Grynbaum, Shane, & Flitter, 2018).

Relationships will develop, and you can't fight Mother Nature. But you can respect the ethics and boundary of the job and alert your editor to relationships that arise. Never cover those with whom you have more than a professional relationship. Your ethics and theirs are on the line.

References

Cano, R. G. (2011). Pulitzer Prize-Winning Columnist Connie Schultz Resigns from *The Plain Dealer* (Updated). September 21. Retrieved June 25, 2018, from http://blog.cleveland.com/metro/2011/09/connie_schultz_resigned_today. html.

Dart Center. (2015). Covering Breaking News: Interviewing Victims and Survivors. October 13. Retrieved June 20, 2018, from https://dartcenter.org/content/covering-breaking-news-interviewing-victims-and-survivors

Farhi, P. (2012). Conn. School Shooting: When Children Are Witnesses, How Should Media Proceed? December 14. Retrieved June 20, 2018, from www. washingtonpost.com/lifestyle/style/conn-school-shooting-when-children-are-witnesses-how-should-media-proceed/2012/12/14/7f128756-462f-11e2-8061-253bccfc7532_story.html?noredirect=on&utm_term=.501010d7ace6.

Grynbaum, M., Shane, S., & Flitter, E. (2018). How an Affair Between a Reporter and a Security Aide Has Rattled Washington Media. June 25. Retrieved from www.nytimes.com/2018/06/24/business/media/james-wolfe-ali-watkins-leaks-reporter.html?hp&action=click&pgtype=Homepage&clickSource=story-heading&module=first-column-region&ion=top-news&WT.nav=top-news.

Peters, J., Belmas, G., & Bobkowski, P. (2017). A Paper Shield? Whether State Privilege Protections Apply to Student Journalists. *Fordham Intellectual Property, Media and Entertainment Law Journal*, *27*(4), 763–801. Retrieved June 20, 2018, from https://ir.lawnet.fordham.edu/iplj/vol27/iss4/2.

Society of Professional Journalists. (n.d.). SPJ Code of Ethics - Society of Professional Journalists. Retrieved from www.spj.org/ethicscode.asp.

11 There Are Stupid Questions—But You Don't Have to Ask Them

As a reporter covering horse racing, I once interviewed a trainer with an entry in a high-profile race—and his horse looked terribly overmatched. She had not won that season, and seemed, on paper, to be far slower that other competitors.

My skepticism was evident when I asked him, "Why did you enter your horse in this race when she seems to have little chance of winning?"

Now, he clearly felt she had a very good chance or he would not have brought her thousands of miles and paid thousands of dollars to enter. And he was furious at my question. His answer was hostile and aggressive, and it did not serve my purposes or his.

He then told everyone he could find that I was an idiot.

I was right his horse was overmatched—she finished last—and the question did need to be asked, but I should have thought ahead to the ways in which he would likely respond to that question.

What about: "You horse has raced in pretty tough company and not had a lot of luck this year, but you obviously believe in her enough to bring her here. What are you seeing in her that others might be missing?"

Yeah, that would have been better.

It's every interviewer's fear—your subject will hear your question and have no doubt it is the dumbest question ever asked. Often, it's not a bad question but rather it is asked badly. Sometimes the question itself is not working. Sports writer Bill Finley says the worst questions are from people who aren't prepared and don't understand the subject:

> For instance, you're interviewing a baseball pitcher having a good year. I've actually heard people say, 'How did you do last year?' Don't ask that question! You have to know that type of thing. What really turns people off is when you know you're asking stupid questions out of ignorance. They're nice enough to give you some their time; you have an obligation to ask intelligent questions.
>
> (Bill Finley, personal interview, 2014)

There are a lot of ways to interview people badly, resulting in bad answers or, even worse, a source who storms off angry.

The following sections focus on some of the challenges you might face—from the minor to the extreme.

Double-Barreled Questions

A lot of concentration goes into answering an interview question, and most people will pick one question to answer—usually the easiest. Separate the ideas, and think in terms of follow-up opportunities that are shaped by the first response.

- **Bad**

  - What are youth hockey's problems, and what are leaders doing to fix them?

- **Better**

  - *Question 1:* What do you think are the biggest challenges facing Columbus youth hockey right now?
  - *Question 2:* You mentioned the limited amount of ice available—how do you see that getting fixed?

Taking Sides

Whether you agree with your subject or think them an idiot is irrelevant to your interview and, subsequently, your story. That means that you have to fight the urge to agree—or disagree—with your source, even when they try to pull you toward their side.

Imagine you were reporting on a Catholic high school that fired a teacher it discovered was a lesbian and living with her partner. The cause cited: cohabitating out of marriage, which is a violation of the diocese moral policy, which the teacher signed.

You are a staunch liberal and believe there should be protection against being fired for sexual orientation. You interview the teacher and, as she tells her side of the story, she asks, "You understand why this is wrong, don't you. Don't you agree this is a travesty."

What happens if you follow your heart and beliefs and say, "Oh my goodness—this is horrible! I can't believe they would do this to you? The students have a petition started for you—that's awesome!"

Result: You have just destroyed any perspective of objectivity, a key tenet of journalism.

Instead, try active listening, a communication technique whereby the listener gives feedback to the speaker about what they have heard: "I hear what you're saying that you feel this was really unfair. Walk me through what happened."

Also consider challenging a source by playing "Devil's advocate," turning the question around and encouraging a more emotional response.

Example: "I hear what you are saying, but let me play Devil's advocate here. Keeping a teacher who goes against the church's teaching could send the wrong message to kids in the school. How would you respond to that?"

Jo Ingles of Ohio Public Radio says, "Guns, abortion—anything controversial—I'm always figuring out what the other side will say. That's what makes good sound" (personal interview, 2018).

Overloading

Questions have to be answerable, and if they are too broad, it will be next to impossible for your source to provide an answer that will be useful to you.

- **Bad**

    - "What do you think about college?"

Why exactly are you asking the question? What is the answer you are seeking for the reader? Narrow the question so they can answer that.

- **Better**

    - "What have you found are the biggest differences between high school and college?"
    - "You picked a college with more than 60,000 students—what has that been like in your freshman year?"
    - "Ohio State switched to semesters from quarters—how has the change impacted you?"

Adding Emotional Weight

Remember, your opinion is not important here, and if you lead a source with your own bias it will, at best, influence their answers. At worst, it could make them angry or upset to the degree it ruins your interview.

Consider this question to the owner of a flower shop: "Our economy has been in the toilet, which means people are not buying frivolous things like flowers. How has that impacted your business?"

You are trying to find out how a business is impacted when people have less disposable income. It's a valid question. But asked this way, you have almost assuredly offended them by calling their business frivolous.

And our economy is not literally in the toilet. You can cite facts and ask the question the same way.

A better way to ask the question: "The Department of Labor said unemployment in this area has been around 9 percent for the past year, which means a lot of people have less disposable income. How has that impacted your business?"

Trigger Words/Phrases

Another way your opinion comes through is with trigger words that can evoke a visceral response in your subject. Consider this question asked on the night of the 2012 election: "Republicans must truly be getting sick of losing so badly on a national scale. What will it take for there to finally be a GOP winner?"

Republicans knew they lost two presidential races in a row; that was not for us to inform them. How about: "Where does the GOP go from here? What do you see on the horizon heading into the 2016 races?"

Theoretically, your source will tell you thoughts related to a course change, but if your source tells you everything is going great and Republicans plan to stay that course, that would be a bigger story!

Interrupting

I know the answer is not quite what you wanted, or you just thought of another, better question, but let sources finish a thought—even if you know you won't use the quote.

Cutting people off while they are talking is disconcerting, and it can make them less likely to fully answer future questions.

And it is just plain rude.

Making Friends

This is an interview—not a matchmaking session. Stay objective and fair, and remember this person is a tool for you to do your job, not a friend in the making.

"I wear my press pass on my neck and remind them no matter how much time we spend together that I am writing this down," Lane DeGregory says. "Sometimes I am wincing when I get something really intimate. I know it's good, and it's what I need, but it's scary and I want to remind people I am writing it down. That's my purpose here" (personal interview, 2018).

But This Is a Conversation

Jennifer Smith Richards of the *Chicago Tribune* recalls listening to an intern at her first job interview, and every single one was "painful." The reason; he had written out a series of questions, and no matter what the response was from his interviewee, he forged ahead with those questions:

> You could tell he was not listening. He hit all the high points. But he missed what was probably a richer story or a better response. You have to listen to what the person is saying. And ask a question based on what they have just said, not just based on what you want to know.
>
> (Jennifer Smith Richards, personal interview, 2018)

Just Plain Ugly

Matt Brown of SB Nation recalls covering his second-ever high school football game while working for the Newark Advocate. It was, in his words, "a bloodbath."

His question to the losing coach: "How do you stay motivated when game is over in the second quarter?"

"The coach thought my questions were so stupid he walked off the field and ignored me," Brown says. "I cannot describe the burning feeling of shame I felt. After that he would only talk to me in locker room where kids were naked" (personal interview, 2018).

Writer Sally Kuzemchak admits she has conducted interviews where she offended the person with her first question, and it's usually because she did not do her homework:

> I didn't do my research well enough, and I might refer to a paper that wasn't theirs or given a colleague credit for something they did. I was just in a rush to kind of report the story. The other day I totally inadvertently offended somebody by phrasing something a specific way and he just went on this rant about how I said it was wrong, and we just didn't we couldn't recover from that. That was a shame, and I think, in that case, I probably didn't spend enough time writing that question out. I was just sort of going

Figure 11.1 Matt Brown of SB Nation said he has never forgotten one of the worst questions he ever asked a losing coach: "How do you stay motivated when game is over in the second quarter?"

Source: Matt Brown

Figure 11.2 Sally Kuzemchak says if she offends someone in an interview it's usually because she did not do her homework.

Source: Sally Kuzemchak

Figure 11.3 Martin Short was a gracious subject when a "Today Show" interview went a bit off course.

Source: Creative Commons/Dominick D

off the cuff, and I hadn't spoken with him before, so I wasn't really familiar with how he was.

(Sally Kuzemchak, personal interview, 2014)

Those examples pale, however, when compared with Kathy Lee Gifford, whose lack of research is now the stuff of legends. She welcomed actor Martin Short to the *Today Show* on May 30, 2012, and turned the conversation to Short's wife, Nancy.

"You and Nancy have one of the greatest marriages of anybody in show business," she said, asking how long they had been together. When Short replied, "Married 36 years," she asked "Still in love?" His reply: "Madly in love."

The only problem? Short's wife had died of cancer years earlier. (Couch, 2012)

Box 11.1 Anatomy of an Interview

Figure 11.4 A two-hour conversation with Hannah Powell, combined with support interviews, led to a decent profile.

Source: Hannah Powell

In 2015 I was hired by *Capital Style* magazine to write a profile on Hannah Powell, who had taken over as director of the successful charter school KIPP Columbus.

My first step was researching Powell, visiting her LinkedIn page and reading other articles written about her. I also researched the school and checked out standardized test scores, press clippings and reviews at various education sites.

I knew the focus of my story would be about how she came to develop her vision for education, and how that vision came to life as part of the school.

I started to think about what I needed to know, which included:

- Who was Hannah and what made her come to this school?
- What made her different than other administrators?
- What were the goals and vision for the school?
- What was her vision for education and how did it manifest in KIPP?
- What were her successes and failures that brought her where she is today.
- Objectively, how do community and education leaders think she is doing?

To answer these questions, I knew I needed to speak to Powell, so that interview was the first I set up. I also needed to speak with members of the KIPP board, who hired her to execute their vision and hers. I also sough to speak to her educational and community partners.

My sources ended up being:

- Hannah Powell
- Abigail Wexner, a prominent Columbus philanthropist and KIPP board member.
- Aimee Kennedy, principal of The Metro School, a Franklin County STEM-focused 7–12 magnet program.
- Rebecca Asmo, chief executive officer of the Boys and Girls Club of Columbus.

Here are the questions I developed for Powell:

1 Tell me about growing up in Springfield—what was your school experience like?
2 Why Wittenberg University? What were you hoping to get out of comm degree?
3 What did you plan to do after?
4 Which shelter did you visit and why?

5   Tell me about an experience there.

6   What do you mean by educational inequity?

7   What was it like deciding to go with Teach for America—reception of family, friends?

8   Did you pick those spots—how LA and Philly. Similar, different?

9   How did you learn about KIPP?

10 Joined as a school leader in 2008—what did that job entail?

11 Work Hard, Be Nice—meaning?

12 What does class look like that helps kids develop knowledge, skills, character and habits to succeed in college?

13 What is possible in public school classrooms—compared with what's happening now.

14 What is wrong with current education model?

15 What was your school experience like—positives and negatives?

16 How you make the leap from Comm to education.

17 Why Teach For America and not law school?

18 What was your impression of Philly schools?

19 What is a reconstitution of charter school?

20 When joined KIPP Journey, not going to well. What was your perception when you took the job?

21 What did you do to turn it around?

22 How determine what are measurable high expectations for academic achievement?

23 What are the formal and informal rewards and consequences?

24 How enforce parental commitment?

25 School day at 7:30-5? Longer than most work days. Rationale?

26 Relentlessly focus on standardized test performance. A lot of backlash on this idea now—how do you address that?

27 College grad the goal—how accommodate students who have other life goals—vocation?

28 How are academics and character connected?

29 Relationship with CCS—shooting down of levy?

30 You were only in classroom a couple of years—how prepare to be an administrator?

31 Racial makeup of school

32 How do we make better schools?

I did not necessarily ask all of these questions, but they were all topics I have found in my research, and I thought might benefit the story.

I scheduled a two-hour block with Powell so I could visit the school, traveling with her to classrooms, and watching her interact with kids and teachers, as well as absorbing the feel of the school. We then spent another hour in her office going through these questions and the follow-ups that came up.

Here is the article that resulted, which appeared in the September 2015 issue of the magazine:

> Hannah Powell bounds down the airy hallways of KIPP Columbus, dressed in a navy KIPP sweatshirt and Kelly green jeans, her blond hair tucked in a loose bun.
>
> "Hi Kipsters! Good Morning! Happy Friday!" she greets kindergarten and first-grade students, all clad in blue KIPP polo shirts as they streamed in for another day of learning to live the motto "Work hard. Be nice."
>
> Hannah trades high fives with a few as they pass her in the hall. One stops for a hug. She tugs the braid of another.
>
> Her strides carry her to the school's dining space, brightly lit by floor-to-ceiling windows that reveal rolling green hills and acres of mature trees. She waves at students in grades five through eight, who have gathered for breakfast. Her next stop is a visit with the Temple Owls of 2027, so named for the university their teacher attended and the date these kindergartners, not even a year into their elementary careers, will graduate from college.
>
> With her Kate Hudson looks and Energizer Bunny enthusiasm, it would be easy to think 34-year-old Hannah was a student teacher, rather than KIPP's head administrator. And with its country club feel, it would be easy to mistake KIPP Columbus for an upscale private school, as opposed to its real mission as a free inner-city charter school for Columbus' underserved population.
>
> That desire to break stereotypes and ensure every child has the tools to be college ready led Hannah to KIPP in the first place, and it helped make it—and she—a model for others to emulate across education.
>
> "Children are ours—every single one of them," she says. "And we have a responsibility to give them the future they deserve."
>
> Recognition of that responsibility began for Hannah during her time as student at Wittenberg University in her hometown

of Springfield, Ohio. She was the first member of her maternal family to enter higher education, and her outgoingness led her to major in Communication.

Her priorities and career perspectives shifted while fulfilling Wittenberg's community service requirement at a homeless shelter, where she came face-to-face with the reality of real poverty—and it was located just a few miles from her own home.

"These kids were 15 minutes away from where I grew up, and they couldn't read, they were hungry, they were tired," she says. "It was incredible. And it made me ask, 'What am I going to do about it?'"

That realization led Hannah, after she earned her undergraduate degree in 2003, to put aside law school goals and instead signed up for Teach for America. Her path was tested, however, when she found herself teaching sixth and seventh grade at Shaw Middle School in a part of Philadelphia few tourists ever reach.

Hannah showed up for her first day, ready to serve, in a new turquois suit, pearl earrings and clipboard to keep organized. She quickly realized she was not in Springfield any more.

"I got my [butt] kicked," she says openly. "I knew what to do, but we weren't speaking the same language. I got cursed out. It was chaos. The other teachers had a bet how long I would last.

"The longest was two weeks."

Hannah called her father, Dan, a pastor, to say she wanted to come home and go to law school after all. But she did not get the expected sympathetic parental response.

"You made commitment, so figure it out," he told her. "If it's not you teaching these kids, who will do it?"

So Hannah rolled up her suit sleeves and dug in. Before her students could learn academics, she had to teach them basics like raising hands to be heard and allowing others to speak uninterrupted in class. She literally arm-wrestled every sixth-grade boy to make a name for herself. She built a community around respect and achievement.

And the more she fell in love with her students, the angrier she got about the inequity she saw in mainstream public education.

"The children in our country, only one of 10 are making it to college, and that's ridiculous," Hannah says. "We have to get really clear and humble ourselves to show what it takes to serve kids the way they deserve. It's not a system."

When her Teach For America commitment ended, Hannah returned to the Buckeye State to work with the Fordham Foundation's Keys to Improving Dayton Schools program, with an eye toward reconstituting failing Ohio charters programs. That led her to seek out successful charters to model— and she found herself repeatedly coming back to the KIPP schools.

San Francisco-based KIPP, an acronym for Knowledge Is Power Programs, is a national collection of K–12 charters created to provide free open enrollment, college-preparatory public schools in underserved areas. It operates under five "pillars," or guiding principles:

1 Measurable high expectations for academic achievement.
2 An expressed commitment by students and families who chose the program.
3 An extended school day.
4 Individualized leadership that guides each KIPP site from inside.
5 A focus on results.

Most importantly, the KIPP schools showed Hannah there was a different way to approach education that put students' needs and goals first.

"I was at KIPP Key in [Washington] D.C. and [a teacher] was working with kids on a book," Hannah recalled. "The way they were talking about the text brought me to tears. They showed the applicability in their lives. They were real and kind to one another. They built off each other's ideas.

"When I walked into KIPP, it was clear what was happening and why. What I saw were people who remember the kids. They made it safe, joyful and inspiring. That was the moment I decided to leave and come to KIPP."

That success, however, was not as evident in KIPP Journey, the west-side elementary school that marked the company's first foray into Columbus. Less than four months after its 2008 opening, it was one-third under capacity—with just over 70 students—and $200,000 over budget. Disruptive kids appeared not to have bought into the school's philosophy. The founding principal resigned in November.

"It was an unmitigated disaster," Hannah says ruefully. "They had high expectation for teaching and learning and behavior that did not show results. They were well-intentioned people, but there were gaps."

In stepped Hannah on Dec. 1 to fill those gaps, though board member Abigail Wexner admits there was little thought at the time that KIPP was unleashing a future educational star.

"We were at a very critical point after our first year of opening," Abigail says. "We had the wrong school leaders. We were not delivering on the promises we had made to the families. We were fortunate Hannah came in to help at that time. We had not narrowed in on her as someone who could lead the larger school. We were considering all options— including closing. We knew we had to recruit an entirely new staff and get the school on track—both the academics and the culture of the school.

"Hannah [proved to be] tenacious and curious and hard working, and the quickest study I have ever met."

Hannah's plan for tackling the challenge involved selecting three to five key aspects to prioritize and work toward improvement. Her primary goals: restablishing the KIPP philosophy among the students and staff, closing the budget deficit, recruiting students, and adjusting lesson plans to meet student needs and academic goals.

She assembled a team of KIPP veterans and others committed to the KIPP philosophy to strengthen the curriculum and solidify the culture. Through their efforts, the student count increased from 50 the first year to 135 the next.

"We can't solve our problems using the same programs we used to create them," she says. "Charters are designed to be incubators of innovation, to be collaborative and synergistic with school districts, to provide choices, to be very responsive to needs of the kids. That's what I was attracted to."

She also partnered with industry and community experts who could use their strengths to make KIPP stronger. Among them was Aimee Kennedy, then principal of The Metro School, a Franklin County STEM-focused 7–12 magnet program. The two met when Hannah toured Metro to get ideas to emulate, and have stayed close through Kennedy's move to lead education philanthropy and STEM learning at Battelle.

"What I learned from Hannah Powell is her philosophy: 'Find a way or make one,'" Aimee says. "She has a vision for kids that is transcendental. She knows what kids can achieve, and she will persist until she makes it happen."

In her Battelle role, Aimee has worked with KIPP teacher training and establishing partnerships to prepare the KIPP kids for jobs that may not yet exist. She says Hannah's ability to seek and utilize help from the best players is what makes her so successful.

"Hannah recognizes she does not have all the answers," Aimee says. "She will not hesitate to bring the right people to the table who have the answers. She asks, 'What kind of equipment do we need to have a 21st century science lab? What are other people doing to get kids to and through college?' She prepares kids for life beyond a diploma.

"Hannah has a gift for engaging people in pointed and difficult conversations, and challenging perception. Every single day, she reminds people they need to be the driving force for kids."

That engagement helped KIPP grow to 300 students by 2011. In 2014 more than 600 students, 60 staff members and 50 teachers moved into its present, palatial home at 2750 Agler Road, which was formerly the Columbus State Community College-owned Bridgeview Golf Course. A guarded gate and white split-rail fencing make the 124-acre, $2.3 million purchase seem more like a Kentucky horse farm than a school.

In 2015, KIPP was home to kindergarten and first grade, as well as fifth through eighth grade. With the new facility will come an expansion next year of three more buildings to accommodate and fill in all grades between kindergarten and 12th grade, welcoming 2,000 students.

It is a big goal, but those who know her best say there is no one better suited to the task than Hannah.

"She has an incredible passion for what she is doing," Rebecca Asmo, chief executive officer of the Boys and Girls Club of Columbus, says. "She will do whatever it takes to get the job done, even in the face of criticism and challenges.

"Ultimately, it's the kids—seeing individual stories of just how kids are impacted when good work is done. That is her motivation."

In addition to her community partners, Hannah also finds motivation and support from her husband, Todd Tuney, who she met through Abigail Wexner when he worked at The Limited. Last year Tuney left City Year, where he had served as director, to become Columbus City Schools' chief of communication and community affairs.

The pair recently settled in the Short North.

Hannah may be settled in her personal life, but she knows there is still much work to be done professionally. No matter how big KIPP grows, Hannah says she is committed to maintaining the quality that treats every student like a potential college student, and follows the PETSYS model of behavior: please, excuse me, thank you, sorry, your welcome and smile.

She makes a promise to every family who commits to KIPP: She will not stop until every child has the chance to find his or her own success.

"I refuse to believe a child is a demographic, or their family, zip code or color dictate their destiny," Hannah says. "Our kids are some of the most inspiring, hopeful, strong people I have ever known. This is … an opportunity to build and create an academic environment to fundamentally transform the lives of a generation to come.

"This can be solved in our lifetime—one kid at a time."

Source: Kraft (2015)

References

Couch, A. (2018). Kathie Lee Gifford Apologizes For Asking Martin Short Why HeStill Loves His Late Wife (Video). June 17. Retrieved June 20, 2018, from www.hollywoodreporter.com/live-feed/kathie-lee-gifford-martin-short-wife-331146.

Kraft, N. (2015). A New Approach. *Capital Style*, September/October, pp. 64–67.

12 Let's Talk

I worked with a man named Ian Fitzsimmons, who is one of the best interviewers in the business. I remember him having [former Cincinnati Bengal's quarterback] Carson Palmer on the air, and as soon as the interview was over, I asked Ian how long he and Carson had known each other. "Oh," answered Ian, "that was my first time ever speaking to him." He had established rapport from the start of his discussion with Carson by asking him about paintball as opposed to football. It set Ian apart from other interviewers. It let Carson know this would not be a typical interview, thus he could not put his mind into cruise control, and Ian got thoughtful answers as a result. And it let Carson talk about something fun, as opposed to, say, the struggles of the Bengals.

(Lori Schmidt, radio reporter, personal interview, 2018)

In her book *Reclaiming Conversation*, MIT researcher Sherry Turkle rejects the idea that communication has died in the online age. Instead, she says, society is talking more than ever—through social media, email, even phones and in person. What we are not doing is talking with each other or listening with any purpose to what each person has to say (Turkle, 2016).

A conversation is a dance. It has ebbs and flows. It can be exciting and boring. But it is a journey that must be taken with companionship, in a world where individual needs and desires have, in many ways, taken precedence over community.

The desire for speed and need to cut to the chase—to just get an answer and move on—has limited our engagement with conversation and it is reflected in the biggest challenge with interviews. Yes, interviewing is intended to obtain information—for without that information we simply have no material with which to write. That is the mechanism of an interview—questions and answers.

But interviewing is more a craft than a practice. It is the most human possible art form, in which scenes are painted with words, and narrative makes stories come to life. It may seem the source is the artist in this scenario,

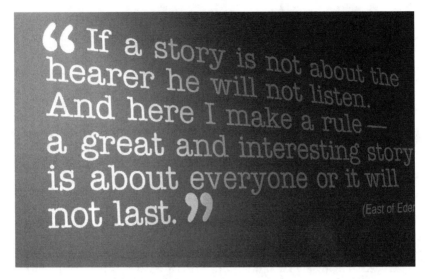

"If a story is not about the hearer he will not listen. And here I make a rule — a great and interesting story is about everyone or it will not last." (East of Eden)

Figure 12.1 This quote from John Steinbeck the at the Steinbeck Center in Salinas, California, is a reminder for all writers that it's the readers that matter.

Source: Creative Commons/Jill Clardy

but in fact he or she is more the paint and canvas. It is the interviewer who wields the brush, asking the right questions, using the right questioning techniques, guiding with a gentle hand to extracting scene after scene.

It is the interviewer who observes with an eye toward painting description with words. It is the interviewer who sees the finished product in its fullest and most complex form.

"Good journalism is, at its essence, good storytelling," Lori Schmidt says:

> Therefore, the best question you can ever ask is, "Can you tell me a story?" Obviously, it's rarely worded that way, but examples of "tell-me-a-story" questions might be, "What was the moment you realized this athlete you're coaching was special?" "How did you celebrate this milestone achievement?" "You said this teammate is a good leader. What's an example of a time she showed leadership?"
>
> (Lori Schmidt, personal interview, 2018)

The guidance provided in this book will provide you with the fundamentals of being a good interviewer. Simple questions will provide the who, what, when, where and why of our story—the facts. But to truly excel at interviewing you need to do more than get the name of the dog. You need to really listen to what people have to say, and to help them see that the value of your interaction is not the meeting itself, but rather the

Figure 12.2 Lori Schmidt says good journalism is, at its essence, good storytelling.
Source: Lori Schmidt

common language and the emotional string you tie to one another for the course of your story. You need to actually care what your source has to say, and care about the story to which they are contributing their narrative and experiences.

To your source, this is not a job—it is their life. Their willingness to share it is a gift to repay with undivided attention and accuracy.

You are ready to go out and start interviewing armed with the knowledge, examples, guidance and support you need. You will ask some terrific questions. You will ask questions that make you want to slap your head in frustration. You will leave some interviews thinking you made magic and leave others thinking, "Why didn't I ask that?"

You can't simply read about interviewing and become a great interviewer. You have to get out in the field and start asking questions. You also have to make mistakes, feel like an idiot, have some source imply or say you are an idiot, and then get back out there and do it again. You are ready to solicit answers. You are ready to be rebuffed and ignored. You are ready to have someone try and manipulate you with a scripted answer and for you to smile politely and move them toward the information you need.

As you have likely noticed, there is a lot of personalization possible in the field of journalism, and your interview style will quickly become individual to you. How you take notes does not matter, so long as you do it accurately and treat people fairly. Your source pool can be wide and varied, provided they are experts on the topics you plan to write.

Interviewing skill is like a muscle. The more you flex and work it, the better and stronger it will get, until you find yourself interviewing people on the bus, at a party, in the doctor's office, and not even realizing it.

That may feel like overkill, but remember that story ideas come from talking to people about what they do and how they do it. The better your questions in every circumstance, and the more you care about the responses, the easier story ideas may come.

"Don't be a jerk," says Holly Zachariah. "Interviewing people and talking to them is all about making a connection. Why would anyone make a connection with me and tell me anything if I'm a jerk? Being a better person translates into making you a better reporter" (personal interview, 2018).

As you turn this final page, start preparing to ask questions the best way you now know how.

Answers—like the name of the dog—await you.

References

Turkle, S. (2016). *Reclaiming Conversation: The Power of Talk in a Digital Age*. New York: Penguin Books.

Resources

Columbia Journalism Review (www.cjr.org)

CJR's mission is to be the intellectual leader in the rapidly changing world of journalism. It is the most respected voice on press criticism, and it shapes the ideas that make media leaders and journalists smarter about their work. Through its fast-turn analysis and deep reporting, CJR is an essential venue not just for journalists, but also for the thousands of professionals in communications, technology, academia, and other fields reliant on solid media industry knowledge.

Dart Center for Journalism and Trauma (https://dartcenter.org)

A resource center and global network of journalists, journalism educators and health professionals dedicated to improving media coverage of trauma, conflict and tragedy. It is a project of Columbia University Graduate School of Journalism in New York City, with international satellite offices in London and Melbourne.

Investigative Reporters and Editors (www.ire.org)

A grassroots nonprofit organization dedicated to improving the quality of investigative reporting.

Journalist's Resource

Based at Based at Harvard's Shorenstein Center on Media, Politics and Public Policy, it examines news topics through a research lens. We curate scholarship relevant to media practitioners, bloggers, educators, students and general readers.

Journalist's Toolbox (www.journaliststoolbox.org)

A collection of resources presented by the Society of Professional Journalists to help journalists better do their jobs and for educators to produce better journalists.

Interviewing Course, News University, by Poynter (www.newsu.org/courses/interview)

This free, self-directed course teaches what you need to know about being a better interviewer and allow you to put those lessons into practice as you learn. With the aid of a virtual coach and a typical encounter with a, not entirely forthcoming source, you'll have the chance to see firsthand how the kinds of questions you pose can stop or start an effective interview.

Other NewsU Classes Offered for a Fee

- The Art of the Interview with Lane DeGregory (www.newsu.org/courses/art-of-the-interview-degregory).
- The Art of the Interview: Master Class with Jacqui Banaszynski (www.newsu.org/masterclass-banaszynski).
- Where's the Feeling? Finding Genuine Emotions in Interviewing (www.newsu.org/courses/find-emotions-interview).

Online News Association (https://journalists.org)

The world's largest association of digital journalists. ONA's mission is to inspire innovation and excellence among journalists to better serve the public. Membership includes journalists, technologists, executives, academics and students who produce news for and support digital delivery systems.

Poynter (www.poynter.com)

Engages with media executives, journalists, technologists and academics to advance newsgathering and teaching journalism, with focus areas including fact-checking, ethics, leadership, innovation and storytelling.

Reporters Committee for Freedom of the Press (www.rcfp.org)

Founded by leading journalists and media lawyers in 1970 when the nation's news media faced an unprecedented wave of government sub-poenas forcing reporters to name confidential sources. Today it provides pro bono legal representation, *amicus curiae* support, and other legal resources to protect First Amendment freedoms and the newsgathering rights of journalists.

Society of Professional Journalists (www.spj.org)

The nation's most broad-based journalism organization, dedicated to encouraging the free practice of journalism and stimulating high standards of ethical behavior.

Index

active learning 114
active listening 72, 78, 137
Adobe Connect 50
advanced search 12
Ambush interview 79
anecdote (anecdotal) 4, 16, 21, 23
angle 6, 7, 11, 24, 29, 73, 96,
    112; see also focus
answers 79, 87, 93, 110–111, 116, 124,
    136, 138, 149, 151, 153–154
Apel, T. 131–134, *132*
apps 12, 31, 37, 39, 50
appearance 97; see also dressing up
Apple, Inc. 12, 20, 120
Apple pencil 39
approaching a source 8–9, 29–30, 128
Asmo, R. 143
Associated Press 9–10, 21, 57–58, 93
athlete time 106
Athletic, The 96, *102*
attribution 39–43, 53; deep background
    43; on background 43; not for 43;
    paraphrase 41–42, 52, 72, 116, 131
audience 52, 93, 101, 110, 113, 121
audio 35, 37–38, 111, 114–120

background 4, 7, 9, 20, 29, 43, 85,
    115, 118–119
beat 13, 31, 63
bell curve 64, 67, 84
Belmas, G. 131
Bernstein, C. 32
bike polo 8
Binkley, C. 1, 21, *22*, 26
Bobkowski, P. 131
body language 2, 48, 50, 52, 61–62,
    72, 81
Boyle, T. 120–122

broadcast *17*, 38, 62, 92, 101, 107, 119,
    120, 122, 128, 133–134
Brown, M. 140, *140*
Brown, S. 134
brush off (blown off) 111
Bull Durham 92
Bump, P. 121

camera position 118
campaign see speeches
Capital Style 142
Car2Go *27*, 27–29
Cartwright, S. 13, *14*
character (characterization) 52, 65, 80,
    130, 144
Charlie Rose syndrome 62
chess *68*, 69, 111
Chicago Tribune 44, 139
children (interviewing) 125–126
Cleveland Browns 97, 99–100
Cleveland Plain Dealer 134
Cleveland.com 97
clubhouse 103
CNN 121
Code of Ethics (Society of Professional
    Journalists) 124, 127, 133
Columbia Journalism Review 155
Columbus Blue Jackets 53, 97, *102*
Columbus Dispatch 1, 13, 41, 67, 82–83,
    99, 127, 129
Columbus Monthly 73, 73
commencement see speeches
comment: declined to 79; did not
    respond to repeated attempts 80; not
    available for 80
common ground 81
compassion 72, 81, 127
computer *35*, 35–36, 38–39, 50

confidential sources *see* unnamed
  sources
conversation (conversational) 1–4, 6, 9,
  29–30, 37–39, 47, 51–52, 58, 61,
  63–65, 74, 76, 78, 81, 84, 95, 103,
  117–120, 122, 132, 139, 142,
  149, 151
Couric, K. *45*
Covey, S. 3
curiosity 59, 125, 128, 133

Dangerfield, R. 18
Dart Center for Journalism and Trauma
  128, 155
data set *20*
Davey, C. 52
Davis, R. 70
deadline 31, 38, 47–48, 51, 80, 131
DeGregory, L. 51, 65, 80, *82*, 84, 87,
  139, 156
demand 59
Devil's advocate 137–138
digital recorder *see* recorder
discouraged 18, 104, 107
distraction 3, 44
dressing up 47; *see also* appearance
Dur, W. 131

electronic *see* audio, video
email 13, 21, 26, 30–31, 42, 50–53, *53*,
  66, 80–81, 99, 134, 151
emotion (emotional) 24, *25*, 71, 81,
  87–88, 92, 94, 96, 100, 102, 110, 127,
  129–130, 137, 153
emotional weight 138
empathy 88, 127, 129
environment 4
equipment 39, 115–116
ethics (ethical) 31, 38, 42, 50–51, 79,
  123, 126, 134, 156
eye contact 4, 34, 36–37, 47, 62, 81

fabrication 131
Facebook 8, 11–13, 80, 106, 133
FaceTime 50
face-to-face 30–31, 49, 106, 146
facial expression 50, 118
fairness 32
fandom 94, 99
Felt, M. (Deep Throat) 32
Ferentz, K. 95
filler (verbal) 114, 117
Finley, B. 103, 136

Fitzsimmons, I. 151
focus 68, 113, 118, 122, 143–144, 147;
  see also angle
Fox News 67
Fox, S. *105*, 105
Frank Sinatra Has a Cold 18
friends, interviewing of 13, 31, 44, 122,
  123, 139

Gates, R. *45*
Gaudi, S. 23
Gita, B. 6
Gifford, K. 142
Golden State Warriors 63, 100
golden rule 48
Google 7–8, 50, 96
Google Voice 50
Grantland 104
Greene, J. 14
Guardian, The 120
Gulotta, M. 71

Hammersley, B. 120
handshake 45, 47, 55
handwriting 35–37, 39
Harden, M. 129
hashtag 12–13
heart, reporting with *82*, 87, 130
Hidden Brain 120
horse racing 136
Hunter, M. 40–41
Huntley, S. 45

implications 72, 128, 133
impropriety 123, 130
Ingles, J. 31, 120, 138
in person 29–31, 42, 46, 48–51, 107, 151
Instagram 11–13, 107
interjections (interrupt, interrupting,
  interruptions) 30, 62, 77, 114,
  117–118, 139, 146
interrogation 85
intimate interview 80
introduction (introduce) 25, 30–31, 47,
  50, 113, 119
iPad 25, 36, 61, 116, *119*
iPhone *37*, 116
iPod 66, 120
investigative reporters and editors 155
Irving, K. 100

Jacobs, K. 45, *73*
James, L. 57–58, *59*, 63, 97, 100

jargon 111
jerk (don't be one) 83, 130, 154
Johnson, J. 53–55, *55*
Journalist's Resource 155
Journalist's Toolbox 156

Kennedy, A. 143, 148–149
Kennedy, G. 121
Kentucky Derby 109
Kuzemchak, S. 64, *141*
The Lantern 30–31

laptop 38–39
lavalier 116, 118
lede 54, 57, 85, 89
Leerhsen, C. 4, 10, 18, 48, 61, 76, 77,
    79, 84, 109–110
legal (legality) 31, 36, 38, 50–51, 128,
    133, 156
lexicon 111
LinkedIn 12, 14, 143
listen (listening) 2–3, 10, 32, 38, 61–64,
    69, 72, 78, 81, 88–89, 97, 101, 103,
    116–118, 120–122, 137, 139, 151–152
Littler, E. 95
location 40, 44, 109, 114–115, 118
locker room 93, 102–103, 140
Love, K. 96, 103
Ludlow, R. 127
Lukan, A. 96, 102
lurker 111

mannerisms 34, 46
March Madness 94
Mariota, M. 104
Marjory Stoneman Douglas school 126
Mattingly, P. 121
McIlroy, R. 104
Media Ethics Division (Association of
    Educators in Journalism and Mass
    Communication) 131
media relations 28, 57, 93–94, 107
meetings 109, *112*, 112–113
Meyer, U. *98*, 104
McClelland, M. 6, 62–63, 77
McEwan, I. 10
MLB Network 92
MP3 50, 120
multimedia 51, 58, 115
muscle (interviewing skill) 154

National Public Radio (NPR) 10, 32, 120
NCAA tournament 105

News University 156
New York Times 20, 32, 42,
    103, 135
no comment 79
Nola.com 40
not an expert 98
notepad (notebook) 1, 34–36, *35*, 39,
    47, 62, 84
notes 5, 7, 26, 34–39, *35, 36*, 48–49,
    52–54, 62, 80, 87, 113, 118, 154

observation(s) 19, 52, 109
Oscars 109
Ohio Public Radio 31, 120, 138
Ohio State University (Ohio State) 14,
    23, 41, 46–47, 52, 82–83, *98*, 99,
    121, 138
off the record 42, 125
on the record 42–43, 129–130
one-on-one 57, 93, 109, 133
online 11–13, 20, 151; *see also* website
Online News Association 156
Oren, P. 51–52, *53*
Owens, A. *17*

Palmer, C. 151
Paul, C. 106
Pearlman, J. 26, 80, 88–90, *90*
Peters, J. 131
phone (calls) 23, 30–31, *37*, 37–38, 42,
    45, 49, 49–51, 90, 111, 151
Pinske, B. 84, *86*
Pinske, M 86, *86*
pitch 26, 29, 31, 80
plagiarism (plagiarize) 42, 124
player time 97, 99, 107
Plesac, D. 92, *95*, 95–97, 99, 101,
    104, 107
podcasting 119–122; audience 121;
    language 122
podium 93, 111
police 1, 19, 21, 23, 42, 45, 73–74, 127,
    131–134
Popovich, G. 106
Porzingis, K. 106
Powell, H. 142–143, 145, 149
Poynter 156
pre-game ritual 99
press box 95; no cheering 95
press conference 96, *98*, 100–102,
    104–105, 107, 109–112, *110, 119*
Prince, T. 105
privilege (reporter's) 131

profile 12, 18–19, 23, 28, 47, 53, *55*, 73–74, 83–84, 88, 106–107, 136, *142*
prompt (prompting) 117
Pulitzer, J. 37
Pulitzer Prize *82*, 84

questions: ahead of time 123; answerable 52, 138; closed-ended 2–3, 60, 109; development 1, 23, 78, 113–114; double-barreled 137; flow 31, 42, 61, 101, 151; follow up 10, 16, 31, 50–52, 61–63, 69–70, 74, 111, 113, 137, 145; good 59, 111, 124; horrible 110; how many 64, 109; lazy 109; leading 60; open-ended 60, 63, 114, 116; order 61–62, 64–65, 93; overloading 138; pre-planning 122; prescreening 17; rally killer 100; sending to source 123; sequence 62; stupid 4, 9, 21, 77, 105, 136, 140; taking sides 137; talk about 104, *105*; two-part 116; ugly 140; worst 3, 65, 69, 74, 105, 136, *140*
quotes (quoted) 1, 2, 4–5, 16, 18, 20–21, 23, 26, 34–35, *36*, 37, 40–42, 52, 58, 60, 62, 64, 68–69, 78, 84, 87, 117, 125, 131, 133, 139

radio 51, 101, 114, *120*, 120–121; *see also* audio
Ramsey, C. 24
reason to return 87
rebooting 78
Reclaiming Conversation 151
recorder (recording) 31, 35, *37*, 37–39, 43, 47, 51, 78, 89, 111, 114–116, 118–119, 125
Reed, T. *102*
relationships 94, 103, 134–135
relentless 87
Reporters Committee for Freedom of the Press 156
research 25, 29, 58, 73–74, 95, 110, 114, 121, 128, 140, 142–144, 155
rinse and repeat 77
Rocker, J. 88–90, *90*

Saffian, S. 6, 10–11, *46*, 46–47, 62
Sandy Hook Elementary School 125
Santa Rosa Press Democrat 41
Sawatsky, J. 59–60, 62
SB Nation 140, *140*
scene 19, 34, 85, 132, 151–152

schlub 48
Schmidt, L. 114, 116, 151–152, *153*
Schock, B. 3, 65
Schultz, C. 134
Schwarz, M. 63
script 10, 69–71, 79, 113
scrum 93, *94*, 102
Sept. 11 (9/11) 71, *72*
Short, M. *141*, 142
silence 77, 78–79, 81
Simon, S. *9*, 10
The 7 Habits of Highly Effective People; Powerful Lessons in Personal Change 3
60 Minutes 79
Skype 50
Smith Richards, J. 44, 67, *67*, 139
Snapchat 11
social media 11–15, *12*, 26, 28, 51, 106–107, 123, 126, 151; *see also* Facebook; Instagram; LinkedIn; Snapchat; Twitter
Society of Professional Journalists 124, 127, 133, 156
soundbites 97, 118
sources: agenda 22, 24, 77, 109, 111, *see also* sources (motivation); dating 134; environmental 19, 21; motivation 32, 124, 131, *see also* sources (agenda); official 13, 17, 19, 24, 28–29, 32, 43, 77, 79, 112; qualified 40; supporting 19, 23; stored 20; unnamed 31–32, 131
sources, personal 21–22; academics 25; average people 25; experts 25, 148, 154; newsmaker obligated for coverage 24; newsmaker seeking coverage 24; primary 3, 22; secondary 24; unintentional newsmaker 24
Spayd, L. 32
speeches 109, 112; campaign 113; commencement 113
Sports Illustrated 10, 77, 79–80, 88, 103
storytelling 92, 152, *153*, 156
Steinbeck, J. *152*
student journalist 34, 51–52, 121, 128
Student Slant 121
surgical strike 67
swivel chair 118

tablet (iPad) 25, 36, 39, 61, 116, *119*
Talese, G. 18
Tape A Call 50
tattoo 80–82

technospeak 30
Temple, J. 126
texting 3, 51
tips and tricks 76
Tortorella, J. *102*
transcribe (transcribing, transcription)
    34–35, 38–39, 49, 118; discomfort
    38; legality (illegality) 38; noise 38,
    44, 114, 118
trigger words 139
tripod 116
Trump, D. 100
trust 32, 65, 80, 128, 133–134
Turkle, S. 151
Tweet (tweeted) 13, 21, 100, *126*
Twitter 11–14, 107, 131
typing 21, 35, 38–39

unethical 79, 123, 125

Valentine's Day 11, 21
Varda, Z. 97
Vardon, J. 97–98
Vedantam, S. 120, *121*
verbatim 5, 34–35, *37*, 41, 61, 117,
    127, 131
Verducci, T. 103
verifiable 34
victim (interviews) 24, 127–129; crime
    1, 21, 23, 24, 131, *132*, 134; disaster

127, 148; empathy 81, 84, 87, 127,
    129; revictimize 127
video 8, 31, 38, 50–51, 95, 114–119,
    115, 132–133

Wallace, B. *49*
Wallace, M. 79
Washington Post 121, 126
Watkins, A. 135
web search 8, 50
website 8, 20
Wexner, A. 143, 148
Wikipedia 20
Williams, J. 67
Winter Olympics 76
Withers, T. 57, *59*, 93, 96,
    100–103
witnesses 1, 12, 127
Wolfe, J. 135
Woodward, B. 32
working backwards 27
wrangling 78

YouTube 8, 11, 80
"Y-Press Power-Of-The-Question
    Project" 10, 59

Zachariah, H. 82, *83*, 88, 127,
    129–130, 154
zoom 50